WILLIAM SHAKESPEARE was born in Stratford-upon-Avon in April 1564, and his birth is traditionally celebrated on April 23. The facts of his life, known from surviving documents, are sparse. He was one of eight children born to John Shakespeare, a merchant of some standing in his community. William probably went to the King's New School in Stratford, but he had no university education. In November 1582, at the age of eighteen, he married Anne Hathaway, eight years his senior, who was pregnant with their first child, Susanna. She was born on May 26, 1583. Twins, a boy, Hamnet (who would die at age eleven), and a girl, Judith, were born in 1585. By 1592 Shakespeare had gone to London, working as an actor and already known as a playwright. A rival dramatist, Robert Greene, referred to him as "an upstart crow, beautified with our feathers." Shakespeare became a principal shareholder and playwright of the successful acting troupe, the Lord Chamberlain's men (later, under James I, called the King's men). In 1599 the Lord Chamberlain's men built and occupied the Globe Theatre in Southwark near the Thames River. Here many of Shakespeare's plays were performed by the most famous actors of his time including Richard Burbage, Will Kempe, and Robert Armin. In addition to his 37 plays, Shakespeare had a hand in others, including *Sir Thomas More* and *The Two Noble Kinsmen*, and he wrote poems, including *Venus and Adonis* and *The Rape of Lucrece*. His 154 sonnets were published, probably without his authorization, in 1609. In 1611 or 1612 he gave up his lodgings in London and devoted more and more of his time to retirement in Stratford, though he continued writing such plays as *The Tempest* and *Henry VIII* until about 1613. He died on April 23, 1616, and was buried in Holy Trinity Church, Stratford. No collected edition of his plays was published during his lifetime, but in 1623 two members of his acting company, John Heminges and Henry Condell, published the great collection now called the First Folio.

Bantam Shakespeare
The Complete Works—29 Volumes
Edited by David Bevington
With forewords by Joseph Papp on the plays

The Poems: Venus and Adonis, The Rape of Lucrece, The
Phoenix and Turtle, A Lover's Complaint,
the Sonnets

Antony and Cleopatra	*The Merchant of Venice*
As You Like It	*A Midsummer Night's Dream*
The Comedy of Errors	*Much Ado about Nothing*
Hamlet	*Othello*
Henry IV, Part One	*Richard II*
Henry IV, Part Two	*Richard III*
Henry V	*Romeo and Juliet*
Julius Caesar	*The Taming of the Shrew*
King Lear	*The Tempest*
Macbeth	*Twelfth Night*

Together in one volume:

Henry VI, Parts One, Two, and Three
King John and Henry VIII
Measure for Measure, All's Well that Ends Well, and
Troilus and Cressida
Three Early Comedies: Love's Labor's Lost, The Two
Gentlemen of Verona, The Merry
Wives of Windsor
Three Classical Tragedies: Titus Andronicus, Timon
of Athens, Coriolanus
The Late Romances: Pericles, Cymbeline, The Winter's
Tale, The Tempest

Two collections:

Four Comedies: The Taming of the Shrew, A Midsummer
Night's Dream, The Merchant of Venice,
Twelfth Night
Four Tragedies: Hamlet, Othello, King Lear, Macbeth

William Shakespeare

A MIDSUMMER NIGHT'S DREAM

Edited by
David Bevington

David Scott Kastan,
James Hammersmith,
and Robert Kean Turner,
Associate Editors

With a Foreword by
Joseph Papp

BANTAM BOOKS

NEW YORK·TORONTO·LONDON·SYDNEY·AUCKLAND

A MIDSUMMER NIGHT'S DREAM

*A Bantam Book / published by arrangement
with Scott, Foresman and Company*

PRINTING HISTORY
Scott, Foresman edition published / January 1980
*Bantam edition, with newly edited text and substantially revised,
edited, and amplified notes, introductions, and other
materials, published / February 1988*
*Valuable advice on staging matters has been
provided by Richard Hosley.*
Collations checked by Eric Rasmussen.
Additional editorial assistance by Claire McEachern.

Library of Congress Cataloging-in-Publication Data

Shakespeare, William, 1564–1616.
   A midsummer night's dream / William Shakespeare; edited by David
Bevington; David Scott Kastan, James Hammersmith, and Robert Kean
Turner, associate editors; with a foreword by Joseph Papp.
      p.   cm.—(A Bantam classic)
   Bibliography: p.
   ISBN 0-553-21300-8 (pbk.)
   I. Bevington, David M.   II. Title.
PR2827.A2B48   1988
822.3'3—dc19   87–24078
                                                          CIP

Published simultaneously in the United States and Canada

*Bantam Books are published by Bantam Books, a division of Bantam
Doubleday Dell Publishing Group, Inc. Its trademark, consisting of the
words "Bantam Books" and the portrayal of a rooster, is Registered in
U.S. Patent and Trademark Office and in other countries. Marca Regis-
trada. Bantam Books, 666 Fifth Avenue, New York, New York 10103.*

PRINTED IN THE UNITED STATES OF AMERICA

O   0 9 8 7 6 5 4 3 2

Contents

Foreword

It's hard to imagine, but Shakespeare wrote all of his plays with a quill pen, a goose feather whose hard end had to be sharpened frequently. How many times did he scrape the dull end to a point with his knife, dip it into the inkwell, and bring up, dripping wet, those wonderful words and ideas that are known all over the world?

In the age of word processors, typewriters, and ballpoint pens, we have almost forgotten the meaning of the word "blot." Yet when I went to school, in the 1930s, my classmates and I knew all too well what an inkblot from the metal-tipped pens we used would do to a nice clean page of a test paper, and we groaned whenever a splotch fell across the sheet. Most of us finished the school day with ink-stained fingers; those who were less careful also went home with ink-stained shirts, which were almost impossible to get clean.

When I think about how long it took me to write the simplest composition with a metal-tipped pen and ink, I can only marvel at how many plays Shakespeare scratched out with his goose-feather quill pen, year after year. Imagine him walking down one of the narrow cobblestoned streets of London, or perhaps drinking a pint of beer in his local alehouse. Suddenly his mind catches fire with an idea, or a sentence, or a previously elusive phrase. He is burning with impatience to write it down—but because he doesn't have a ballpoint pen or even a pencil in his pocket, he has to keep the idea in his head until he can get to his quill and parchment.

He rushes back to his lodgings on Silver Street, ignoring the vendors hawking brooms, the coaches clattering by, the piteous wails of beggars and prisoners. Bounding up the stairs, he snatches his quill and starts to write furiously, not even bothering to light a candle against the dusk. "To be, or not to be," he scrawls, "that is the—." But the quill point has gone dull, the letters have fattened out illegibly, and in the middle of writing one of the most famous passages in the history of dramatic literature, Shakespeare has to stop to sharpen his pen.

Taking a deep breath, he lights a candle now that it's dark, sits down, and begins again. By the time the candle has burned out and the noisy apprentices of his French Huguenot landlord have quieted down, Shakespeare has finished Act 3 of *Hamlet* with scarcely a blot.

Early the next morning, he hurries through the fog of a London summer morning to the rooms of his colleague Richard Burbage, the actor for whom the role of Hamlet is being written. He finds Burbage asleep and snoring loudly, sprawled across his straw mattress. Not only had the actor performed in *Henry V* the previous afternoon, but he had then gone out carousing all night with some friends who had come to the performance.

Shakespeare shakes his friend awake, until, bleary-eyed, Burbage sits up in his bed. "Dammit, Will," he grumbles, "can't you let an honest man sleep?" But the playwright, his eyes shining and the words tumbling out of his mouth, says, "Shut up and listen—tell me what you think of *this*!"

He begins to read to the still half-asleep Burbage, pacing around the room as he speaks. ". . . Whether 'tis nobler in the mind to suffer the slings and arrows of outrageous fortune—"

Burbage interrupts, suddenly wide awake, "That's excellent, very good, 'the slings and arrows of outrageous fortune,' yes, I think it will work quite well. . . ." He takes the parchment from Shakespeare and murmurs the lines to himself, slowly at first but with growing excitement.

The sun is just coming up, and the words of one of Shakespeare's most famous soliloquies are being uttered for the first time by the first actor ever to bring Hamlet to life. It must have been an exhilarating moment.

Shakespeare wrote most of his plays to be performed live by the actor Richard Burbage and the rest of the Lord Chamberlain's men (later the King's men). Today, however, our first encounter with the plays is usually in the form of the printed word. And there is no question that reading Shakespeare for the first time isn't easy. His plays aren't comic books or magazines or the dime-store detective novels I read when I was young. A lot of his sentences are complex. Many of his words are no longer used in our everyday speech. His profound thoughts are often condensed into poetry, which is not as straightforward as prose.

Yet when you hear the words spoken aloud, a lot of the language may strike you as unexpectedly modern. For Shakespeare's plays, like any dramatic work, weren't really meant to be read; they were meant to be spoken, seen, and performed. It's amazing how lines that are so troublesome in print can flow so naturally and easily when spoken.

I think it was precisely this music that first fascinated me. When I was growing up, Shakespeare was a stranger to me. I had no particular interest in him, for I was from a different cultural tradition. It never occurred to me that his plays might be more than just something to "get through" in school, like science or math or the physical education requirement we had to fulfill. My passions then were movies, radio, and vaudeville—certainly not Elizabethan drama.

I was, however, fascinated by words and language. Because I grew up in a home where Yiddish was spoken, and English was only a second language, I was acutely sensitive to the musical sounds of different languages and had an ear for lilt and cadence and rhythm in the spoken word. And so I loved reciting poems and speeches even as a very young child. In first grade I learned lots of short nature verses— "Who has seen the wind?," one of them began. My first foray into drama was playing the role of Scrooge in Charles Dickens's *A Christmas Carol* when I was eight years old. I liked summoning all the scorn and coldness I possessed and putting them into the words, "Bah, humbug!"

From there I moved on to longer and more famous poems and other works by writers of the 1930s. Then, in junior high school, I made my first acquaintance with Shakespeare through his play *Julius Caesar*. Our teacher, Miss McKay, assigned the class a passage to memorize from the opening scene of the play, the one that begins "Wherefore rejoice? What conquest brings he home?" The passage seemed so wonderfully theatrical and alive to me, and the experience of memorizing and reciting it was so much fun, that I went on to memorize another speech from the play on my own.

I chose Mark Antony's address to the crowd in Act 3,

scene 2, which struck me then as incredibly high drama.
Even today, when I speak the words, I feel the same thrill I
did that first time. There is the strong and athletic Antony
descending from the raised pulpit where he has been speaking, right into the midst of a crowded Roman square. Holding the torn and bloody cloak of the murdered Julius
Caesar in his hand, he begins to speak to the people of
Rome:

> If you have tears, prepare to shed them now.
> You all do know this mantle. I remember
> The first time ever Caesar put it on;
> 'Twas on a summer's evening in his tent,
> That day he overcame the Nervii.
> Look, in this place ran Cassius' dagger through.
> See what a rent the envious Casca made.
> Through this the well-belovèd Brutus stabbed,
> And as he plucked his cursèd steel away,
> Mark how the blood of Caesar followed it,
> As rushing out of doors to be resolved
> If Brutus so unkindly knocked or no;
> For Brutus, as you know, was Caesar's angel.
> Judge, O you gods, how dearly Caesar loved him!
> This was the most unkindest cut of all . . .

I'm not sure now that I even knew Shakespeare had written a lot of other plays, or that he was considered "time-
less," "universal," or "classic"—but I knew a good speech
when I heard one, and I found the splendid rhythms of
Antony's rhetoric as exciting as anything I'd ever come
across.

Fifty years later, I still feel that way. Hearing good actors
speak Shakespeare gracefully and naturally is a wonderful
experience, unlike any other I know. There's a satisfying
fullness to the spoken word that the printed page just can't
convey. This is why seeing the plays of Shakespeare performed live in a theater is the best way to appreciate them.
If you can't do that, listening to sound recordings or watch-
ing film versions of the plays is the next best thing.

But if you do start with the printed word, use the play as a
script. Be an actor yourself and say the lines out loud. Don't

worry too much at first about words you don't immediately understand. Look them up in the footnotes or a dictionary, but don't spend too much time on this. It is more profitable (and fun) to get the sense of a passage and sing it out. Speak naturally, almost as if you were talking to a friend, but be sure to enunciate the words properly. You'll be surprised at how much you understand simply by speaking the speech "trippingly on the tongue," as Hamlet advises the Players.

You might start, as I once did, with a speech from *Julius Caesar,* in which the tribune (city official) Marullus scolds the commoners for transferring their loyalties so quickly from the defeated and murdered general Pompey to the newly victorious Julius Caesar:

> Wherefore rejoice? What conquest brings he home?
> What tributaries follow him to Rome
> To grace in captive bonds his chariot wheels?
> You blocks, you stones, you worse than senseless
>   things!
> O you hard hearts, you cruel men of Rome,
> Knew you not Pompey? Many a time and oft
> Have you climbed up to walls and battlements,
> To towers and windows, yea, to chimney tops,
> Your infants in your arms, and there have sat
> The livelong day, with patient expectation,
> To see great Pompey pass the streets of Rome.

With the exception of one or two words like "wherefore" (which means "why," not "where"), "tributaries" (which means "captives"), and "patient expectation" (which means patient waiting), the meaning and emotions of this speech can be easily understood.

From here you can go on to dialogues or other more challenging scenes. Although you may stumble over unaccustomed phrases or unfamiliar words at first, and even fall flat when you're crossing some particularly rocky passages, pick yourself up and stay with it. Remember that it takes time to feel at home with anything new. Soon you'll come to recognize Shakespeare's unique sense of humor and way of saying things as easily as you recognize a friend's laughter.

And then it will just be a matter of choosing which one of Shakespeare's plays you want to tackle next. As a true fan of his, you'll find that you're constantly learning from his plays. It's a journey of discovery that you can continue for the rest of your life. For no matter how many times you read or see a particular play, there will always be something new there that you won't have noticed before.

Why do so many thousands of people get hooked on Shakespeare and develop a habit that lasts a lifetime? What can he really say to us today, in a world filled with inventions and problems he never could have imagined? And how do you get past his special language and difficult sentence structure to understand him?

The best way to answer these questions is to go see a live production. You might not know much about Shakespeare, or much about the theater, but when you watch actors performing one of his plays on the stage, it will soon become clear to you why people get so excited about a playwright who lived hundreds of years ago.

For the story—what's happening in the play—is the most accessible part of Shakespeare. In *A Midsummer Night's Dream*, for example, you can immediately understand the situation: a girl is chasing a guy who's chasing a girl who's chasing another guy. No wonder *A Midsummer Night's Dream* is one of the most popular of Shakespeare's plays: it's about one of the world's most popular pastimes— falling in love.

But the course of true love never did run smooth, as the young suitor Lysander says. Often in Shakespeare's comedies the girl whom the guy loves doesn't love him back, or she loves him but he loves someone else. In *The Two Gentlemen of Verona*, Julia loves Proteus, Proteus loves Sylvia, and Sylvia loves Valentine, who is Proteus's best friend. In the end, of course, true love prevails, but not without lots of complications along the way.

For in all of his plays—comedies, histories, and tragedies—Shakespeare is showing you human nature. His characters act and react in the most extraordinary ways—and sometimes in the most incomprehensible ways. People are always trying to find motivations for what a character does. They ask, "Why does Iago want to destroy Othello?"

The answer, to me, is very simple—because that's the way Iago is. That's just his nature. Shakespeare doesn't explain his characters; he sets them in motion—and away they go. He doesn't worry about whether they're likable or not. He's interested in interesting people, and his most fascinating characters are those who are unpredictable. If you lean back in your chair early on in one of his plays, thinking you've figured out what Iago or Shylock (in *The Merchant of Venice*) is up to, don't be too sure—because that great judge of human nature, Shakespeare, will surprise you every time.

He is just as wily in the way he structures a play. In *Macbeth*, a comic scene is suddenly introduced just after the bloodiest and most treacherous slaughter imaginable, of a guest and king by his host and subject, when in comes a drunk porter who has to go to the bathroom. Shakespeare is tickling your emotions by bringing a stand-up comic on-stage right on the heels of a savage murder.

It has taken me thirty years to understand even some of these things, and so I'm not suggesting that Shakespeare is immediately understandable. I've gotten to know him not through theory but through practice, the practice of the *living* Shakespeare—the playwright of the theater.

Of course the plays are a great achievement of dramatic literature, and they should be studied and analyzed in schools and universities. But you must always remember, when reading all the words *about* the playwright and his plays, that *Shakespeare's* words came first and that in the end there is nothing greater than a single actor on the stage speaking the lines of Shakespeare.

Everything important that I know about Shakespeare comes from the practical business of producing and directing his plays in the theater. The task of classifying, criticizing, and editing Shakespeare's printed works I happily leave to others. For me, his plays really do live on the stage, not on the page. That is what he wrote them for and that is how they are best appreciated.

Although Shakespeare lived and wrote hundreds of years

ago, his name rolls off my tongue as if he were my brother. As a producer and director, I feel that there is a professional relationship between us that spans the centuries. As a human being, I feel that Shakespeare has enriched my understanding of life immeasurably. I hope you'll let him do the same for you.

♣

You may be a corporate executive or a plain everyday wage slave, a brilliant student or a high-school dropout, eight years old or eighty-plus—but dollars to doughnuts you'll laugh your head off at the antics of Nick Bottom and company in *A Midsummer Night's Dream.*

A group of workingmen meet in a wood (that is also, unbeknownst to them, an enchanted fairyland) and set out to rehearse a play. All of them are shy and modest, with one large exception: Nick Bottom. He is an arrogant, pushy, pompous bully, an egotistical know-it-all—in plain words, a big ass.

But he gets his comeuppance. First we see him actually transformed into an ass through a spell cast by a mischievous wood sprite called Puck; then we see him adored by the beautiful and sexy Queen of the Fairies, Titania, who has been bewitched by her jealous lover, Oberon; and finally we see him awakened from his midsummer night's dream. Typically, in calling it "Bottom's Dream," he takes the credit away from his creator, William Shakespeare.

Two sets of desperate lovers chase each other through the forest, while two magical monarchs, Titania and Oberon, contend for supremacy of the leafy kingdom. To add to the magic, tiny wood creatures abound, with such names as Peaseblossom, Cobweb, Mote, and Mustardseed. Along the way we light upon some of Shakespeare's loveliest poetry— such as Oberon's description of a white blossom turning "purple with love's wound."

And, in the midst of all this enchantment of love and passion, Nick Bottom and his "hempen homespuns"—Quince, Snug, Flute, and Starveling—press on with their hilarious efforts to make a play. The mingling of all these is what makes *A Midsummer Night's Dream* Shakespeare's most captivating comedy.

JOSEPH PAPP

JOSEPH PAPP GRATEFULLY ACKNOWLEDGES THE HELP OF ELIZABETH KIRKLAND IN PREPARING THIS FOREWORD

A MIDSUMMER NIGHT'S DREAM

Introduction

A Midsummer Night's Dream (c. 1594–1595) belongs to the
period of transition from Shakespeare's experimental, imi-
tative comedy to his mature, romantic, philosophical, festive vein. In its lighthearted presentation of love's
tribulations, the play resembles Shakespeare's earlier comedies. The two sets of young lovers (Lysander and Hermia,
Demetrius and Helena), scarcely distinguishable one from
the other, are conventional figures. In them we find
scarcely a hint of the profound self-discovery experienced
by Beatrice and Benedick *(Much Ado about Nothing)* or Ro-
salind and Orlando *(As You Like It)*. At the same time, this
play develops the motif of love as an imaginative journey
from reality into a fantasy world created by the artist, ending in a return to a reality that has itself been partly transformed by the experience of the journey. (Shakespeare gives
us an earlier hint of such an imaginary sylvan landscape in
The Two Gentlemen of Verona.) This motif, with its contrasting worlds of social order and imaginative escape, re-
mained an enduring vision for Shakespeare to the very last.

In construction, *A Midsummer Night's Dream* is a skillful
interweaving of four plots involving four groups of characters: the court party of Theseus, the four young lovers, the
fairies, and the "rude mechanicals" or would-be actors. Felix Mendelssohn's incidental music for the play evokes the
contrasting textures of the various groups: Theseus' hunting horns and ceremonial wedding marches, the lovers'
soaring and throbbing melodies, the fairies' pianissimo
staccato, the tradesmen's clownish bassoon. Moreover,
each plot is derived from its own set of source materials.
The action involving Theseus and Hippolyta, for example,
owes several details to Thomas North's translation (1579) of
Plutarch's *Lives of the Noble Grecians and Romans*, to
Chaucer's "Knight's Tale" and perhaps to his *Legend of Good
Women*, and to Ovid's *Metamorphoses* (in the Latin text or
in William Golding's popular Elizabethan translation). The
lovers' story, meanwhile, is Italianate and Ovidian in tone,
and also in the broadest sense follows the conventions of
plot in Plautus' and Terence's Roman comedies, although

no particular source is known. Shakespeare's rich fairy lore, by contrast, is part folk tradition and part learned. Although he certainly needed no books to tell him about mischievous spirits that could prevent churned milk from turning to butter, for instance, Shakespeare might have borrowed Oberon's name either from the French romance *Huon of Bordeaux* (translated into English by 1540), or from Robert Greene's play *James IV* (c. 1591), or from Edmund Spenser's *The Faerie Queen*, 2.10.75–76 (1590). Similarly, he may have taken Titania's name from the *Metamorphoses*, where it is used as an epithet for both Diana and Circe. Finally, for Bottom the weaver and company, Shakespeare's primary inspiration was doubtless his own theatrical experience, although even here he is indebted to Ovid for the story of Pyramus and Thisbe, and probably to Apuleius' *Golden Ass* (translated by William Adlington, 1566) for Bottom's transformation.

Each of the four main plots in *A Midsummer Night's Dream* contains one or more pairs of lovers whose happiness has been frustrated by misunderstanding or parental opposition. Theseus and Hippolyta, once enemies in battle, become husband and wife; and their court marriage, constituting the overplot of the play, provides a framework for other dramatic actions that similarly oscillate between conflict and harmony. In fact, Theseus' actions are instrumental in setting in motion and finally resolving the tribulations of the other characters. In the beginning of the play, for example, the lovers flee from Theseus' Athenian law; at the end, they are awakened by him from their dream. The king and queen of fairies come to Athens to celebrate Theseus' wedding, but quarrel with each other because Oberon has long been partial to Hippolyta, and Titania partial to Theseus. The Athenian tradesmen go off into the forest to rehearse their performance of "Pyramus and Thisbe" in anticipation of the wedding festivities.

The tragic love story of Pyramus and Thisbe, although it seems absurdly ill-suited for a wedding, simply reinforces by contrast the universal accord reuniting the other couples. This accord is, to be sure, stated in terms of male conquest of the female. Theseus, who originally won the Amazonian Hippolyta with his sword, doing her injuries, finally becomes the devoted husband. Hippolyta, legendary figure of woman's self-assertive longing to dominate the male, emerges as the happily married wife. The reconciliation of Oberon and Titania, meanwhile, reinforces this hierarchy of male over female. Having taught Titania a lesson for trying to keep a changeling boy from him, Oberon relents and eventually frees Titania from her enchantment. Thus, the occasion of Theseus' wedding both initiates and brings to an end the difficulties that have beset the drama's various couples.

Despite Theseus' cheerful preoccupation with marriage, his court embodies at first a stern attitude toward young love. As administrator of the law, Theseus must accede to the remorseless demands of Hermia's father, Egeus. The inflexible Athenian law sides with parentage, age, male dominance, wealth, and position against youth and romantic choice in love. The penalties are harsh: death or perpetual virginity—and virginity is presented in this comedy (despite the nobly chaste examples of Christ, Saint Paul, and Queen Elizabeth) as a fate worse than death. Egeus is a familiar type, the interfering parent found in the Roman comedy of Plautus and Terence (and in Shakespeare's *Romeo and Juliet*). Indeed, the lovers' story is distantly derived from Roman comedy, which conventionally celebrated the triumph of young love over the machinations of age and wealth. Lysander reminds us that "the course of true love never did run smooth," and he sees its enemies as being chiefly external: the conflicting interests of parents or friends; mismating with respect to years and blood; war; death; sickness (1.1.134–142). This description clearly applies to "Pyramus and Thisbe," and it is tested by the action of *A Midsummer Night's Dream* as a whole (as well as by other early Shakespearean plays, such as *Romeo and Juliet*). The archetypal story, whether ending happily or sadly, is an evocation of love's difficulties in the face of social hostility and indifference.

While Shakespeare uses several elements of Roman comedy in setting up the basic conflicts of his drama, he also introduces important modifications from the beginning. For example, he discards one conventional confrontation of classical and neoclassical comedy in which the heroine must choose between an old, wealthy suitor supported by her family and the young but impecunious darling of her heart. Lysander is equal to his rival in social position, income, and attractiveness. Egeus' demand, therefore—that Hermia marry Demetrius rather than Lysander—seems simply arbitrary and unjust. Shakespeare emphasizes in this way the irrationality of Egeus' harsh insistence on being obeyed and Theseus' rather complacent acceptance of the law's inequity. Spurned by an unfeeling social order, Lysander and Hermia are compelled to elope. To be sure, in the end Egeus proves to be no formidable threat; even he must admit the logic of permitting the lovers to couple as they ultimately desire. Thus, the obstacles to love are from the start seen as fundamentally superficial and indeed almost whimsical. Egeus is as heavy a villain as we are likely to find in this jeu d'esprit. Moreover, the very irrationality of his position prepares the way for an ultimate resolution of the conflict. Nevertheless, by the end of the first act the supposedly rational world of conformity and duty, by its customary insensitivity to youthful happiness, has set in motion a temporary escape to a fantasy world where the law cannot reach.

In the forest, all the lovers—including Titania and Bottom—undergo a transforming experience engineered by the mischievous Puck. This experience demonstrates the universal power of love, which can overcome the queen of fairies as readily as the lowliest of men. It also suggests the irrational nature of love and its affinity to enchantment, witchcraft, and even madness. Love is seen as an affliction taken in through the frail senses, particularly the eyes. When it strikes, the victim cannot choose but to embrace the object of his infatuation. By his amusing miscalculations, Puck shuffles the four lovers through various permutations with mathematical predictability. First, two gentlemen compete for one lady, leaving the second lady sadly unrequited in love; then everything is at cross-purposes, with each gentleman pursuing the lady who is in love with the other man; then the two gentlemen compete for the lady they both previously ignored. Finally, of course, Jack shall have his Jill—whom else should he have? The couples are properly united, as they evidently were at some time prior to the commencement of the play, when Demetrius had been in love with Helena, and Lysander and Hermia had courted each other.

We sense that Puck is by no means unhappy about his knavish errors. "Lord, what fools these mortals be!" Along with the other fairies in this play, Puck takes his being and his complex motivation from many denizens of the invisible world. As the agent of all-powerful love, Puck compares himself to Cupid. The love juice he administers comes from Cupid's flower, "love-in-idleness." Like Cupid, Puck acts at the behest of the gods, and yet he wields a power that the chiefest gods themselves cannot resist. Essentially, however, Puck is less a classical love deity than a prankish folk spirit, such as we find in every folklore: gremlin, leprechaun, hobgoblin, and the like. Titania's fairies recognize Puck as one who, for example, can deprive a beer barrel of its yeast so that it spoils rather than ferments. Puck characterizes himself as a practical joker, pulling stools out from under old ladies.

Folk wisdom imagines the inexplicable and unaccountable events in life to be caused by invisible forces who laugh at man's discomfiture and mock him for mere sport. Puck is related to these mysterious forces dwelling in nature who must be placated with gifts and ceremonies. Although Shakespeare restricts Puck to a benign sportive role in dealing with the lovers or with Titania, the actual folk legends about Puck mentioned in this play are frequently disquieting. Puck is known to "mislead night-wanderers, laughing at their harm"; indeed, he demonstrates as much with Demetrius and Lysander, engineering a confrontation that greatly oppresses the lovers even though we perceive the sportful intent. At the play's end, Puck links himself and his fellows with the ghoulish apparitions of death and night: wolves howling at the moon, screech owls, shrouds, gaping graves. Associations of this sort go beyond mere sportiveness to witchcraft and demonology involving spirits rising from the dead. Even Oberon's assurance that the fairies will bless all the marriages of this play, shielding their progeny against mole, harelip, or other birth defects, carries the implication that such misfortunes can be caused by offended spirits. The magic of this play is thus explicitly related to deep irrational powers and forces capable of doing great harm, although of course the spirit of comedy keeps such veiled threats safely at a distance in *A Midsummer Night's Dream*.

Oberon and Titania, in their view of the relationship between gods and men, reflect yet another aspect of the fairies' spiritual ancestry—one more nearly related to the gods and goddesses of the world of Greek mythology. The king and queen of fairies assert that, because they are immortal, their regal quarrels in love must inevitably have dire consequences on earth, either in the love relationship of Theseus and Hippolyta or in the management of the weather. Floods, storms, diseases, and sterility abound, "And this same progeny of evils comes / From our debate, from our dissension; / We are their parents and original" (2.1.115–117). Even though this motif of the gods' quarreling over human affairs is Homeric or Virgilian in conception, the motif in this lighthearted play is more nearly mock-epic than truly epic. The consequences of the gods' anger are simply mirth-provoking, most of all in Titania's love affair with Bottom the weaver.

The story of Bottom and Titania is recognizably a metamorphosis in a playfully classical mode, a love affair between a god and an earthly creature, underscoring man's dual nature. Bottom himself becomes half man and half beast, although he is ludicrously unlike the centaurs, mermaids, and other half-human beings of classical mythology. Whereas the head should be the aspiring part of him and his body the bestial part, Bottom wears an ass's head on his shoulders. His very name suggests the solid nature of his fleshly being (bottom is appropriately also a weaving term). He and Titania represent the opposites of flesh and spirit, miraculously yoked for a time in a twofold vision of man's absurd and ethereal nature.

A play bringing together fairies and mortals inevitably raises questions of illusion and reality. These questions reach their greatest intensity in the presentation of "Pyramus and Thisbe." This play within a play focuses our attention on the familiarly Shakespearean metaphor of art as illusion, and of the world itself as a stage on which men and women are merely players. As Theseus observes, apologizing for the ineptness of the tradesmen's performance, "The best in this kind are but shadows" (5.1.210). That is, Shakespeare's own play is of the same order of reality as Bottom's play. Puck too, in his epilogue, invites any spectator offended by Shakespeare's play to dismiss it as a mere

 for an unusually gorgeous entry near the end of
featured Juno in a machine drawn by peacocks
ding tails, a Chinese garden, six monkeys coming
ng the trees, and six moving pedestals, all of
 followed by a grand dance for the finale. The
t consolidation of England's only two licensed
panies into one made possible the large cast and
needed to mount so lavish a display.

rrick's *The Fairies*, at the Theatre Royal, Drury
55, continued the musical tradition, its prologue
ously attributing the play to "Signor Shake-
It disposed of the Athenian tradesmen entirely,
 their performance of "Pyramus and Thisbe,"
with only the fairies and the four young lovers,
ome twenty-eight songs with lyrics by John Dry-
nd Waller, John Milton (from his *L'Allegro*), and
speare. When Garrick tried a more fully oper-
n of *A Midsummer Night's Dream* in 1763, this
thirty-three songs, it lasted exactly one night,
attempt to salvage some parts of it under the title
Tale did better. This adaptation included Bottom
lows together with their play, but left out the
rs as well as Theseus and Hippolyta. Frederic
in his production at the Theatre Royal, Covent
 1816, provided music by Thomas Arne and
 its sixteen songs, eliminated the scene with
Act 1, transposed "Pyramus and Thisbe" to the
etterton had done, and concluded with a grand
Theseus' legendary triumphs: his defeat of the
his finding his way through the labyrinth with
aelp, his killing the Minotaur, his sailing with the
in search of the Golden Fleece, and still more.
adelssohn's well-known musical score for Shake-
ay, then, follows a long tradition of musical elab-
endelssohn's complete score was first used by
ck in a production at the Neues Palais in Pots-
3 (the overture having been written in 1826 and
in England by Alfred Bunn in a production at
 in 1833). It soon became standard fare, since it
o well, in nineteenth-century terms, the contrast
e playful fairies, the bumptious tradesmen, the
seus and Hippolyta, and the romantic lovers.

dream—as, indeed, the play's very title suggests. Theseus goes even further, linking dream to the essence of imaginative art, although he does so in a clearly critical and rather patronizing way. The artist, he says, is like the madman or the lover in his frenzy of inspiration, giving "to airy nothing / A local habitation and a name" (5.1.16–17). Artistic achievements are too unsubstantial for Theseus; from his point of view they are the products of mere fantasy and irrationality, mere myths or fairy stories or old wives' tales. Behind this critical persona defending the "real" world of his court, however, we can hear Shakespeare's characteristically self-effacing defense of "dreaming."

"Pyramus and Thisbe," like the larger play surrounding it, attempts to body forth "the forms of things unknown." The play within the play gives us personified moonshine, a speaking wall, and an apologetic lion. Of course it is an absurdly bad play, full of lame epithets, bombastic alliteration, and bathos. In part Shakespeare is here satirizing the abuses of a theater he had helped reform. The players' chosen method of portraying imaginative matters is ridiculous, and calls forth deliciously wry comments from the courtly spectators onstage: "Would you desire lime and hair to speak better?" (5.1.164–165). At the same time, those spectators onstage are actors in our play. Their sarcasms render them less sympathetic in our eyes; we see that their kind of sophistication is as restrictive as it is illuminating. Bottom and his friends have conceived moonshine and lion as they did because these simple men are so responsive to the terrifying power of art. A lion might frighten the ladies and get the men hanged. Theirs is a primitive faith, naive but strong, and in this sense it contrasts favorably with the jaded rationality of the court party. Theseus' valuable reminder, that all art is only "illusion," is thus juxtaposed with Bottom's insistence that imaginative art has a reality of its own.

Theseus above all embodies the sophistication of the court in his description of art as a frenzy of seething brains. Genially scoffing at "These antique fables" and "these fairy toys" (5.1.3), he is unmoved by the lovers' account of their dreamlike experience. Limited by his own skepticism, Theseus has never experienced the enchantment of the forest. Even Bottom can claim more than that, for he has been the lover of the queen of fairies; and although his language cannot adequately describe the experience, Bottom will see it made into a ballad called "Bottom's Dream." Shakespeare leaves the status of his fantasy world deliberately complex; Theseus' lofty denial of dreaming is too abrupt. Even if the Athenian forest world can be made only momentarily substantial in the artifact of Shakespeare's play, we as audience respond to its tantalizing vision. We emerge back into our lives wondering if the fairies were "real"; that is, we are puzzled by the relationship of these artistic symbols to the tangible concreteness of our daily existence. Unless our perceptions have been thus enlarged by sharing in the author's dream, we have not surrendered to the imaginative experience.

A Midsummer Nigh
in Performa

Two rival staging traditions vie for
mance history of *A Midsummer*
stresses the musical and magical q
fairy enchantment, the gossamer ill
other, more disenchanting traditio
of the forest, the degrading aspect
flict between the sexes, and the bre
sion. The first tradition, althoug
supreme for three centuries and re
twentieth century, has had to conter
more radical vision of disillusionr
we are able to respond to both an
differences a debate about the pla

During the seventeenth-century
the closing of its theaters, *A Midsu*
kept alive in the form of a farcical
Merry Conceited Humours of Botto
phasized the clownish antics of
The full play itself did not make
the Restoration era until Thomas
of a spectacular operatic version
cell. Under the title of *The Fairy (*
and was billed as "an opera repre
atre." Shakespeare's text was rea
room for elaborate entries at the
of Italian *intermedii*. At the end
woodland scene was transforme
toes, arches, and walks adorned
provide an elaborate setting fo
dance by the followers of Night.
ons, part of the movable scener
bridge over a river, forming an a
dience could see swimming in t
accompaniment, two swans wh
selves into dancing fairies. "F
moved to Act 3, just before the tr

mak
Act
with
from
whic
then
actin
resou
Da
Lane,
self-c
spear
along
and d
provic
den, E
even
atic ve
time
thoug
of *A F*
and hi
young
Reynol
Garder
others
Helena
forest a
pageant
Amazon
Ariadne
Argonau
Felix N
speare's
oration.
Ludwig
dam in 1
used firs
Drury La
expresse
between
stately T

Along with musical elaboration, an increasing tendency in nineteenth-century performances was toward lavishness and verisimilitude in set designs and costumes. The production of Madame Lucia Vestris and Charles Matthews at Covent Garden in 1840, though it restored much of the play that had been cut in earlier musical versions, indulged in numerous songs (fourteen this time, as well as Mendelssohn's overture, "Wedding March," and other incidental music), and spared no expense in creating stage spectacle. During Act 3 the moon sank gradually, its rays disappearing from the tops of the trees until daylight arrived. Act 5 featured staircases, a hall of statues, a gallery along the back of the stage, and Parisian lanterns of various colors for the fairies to carry. The fairies were clad in virgin white, with immaculate silk stockings. Nothing threatening was to be found in this wholesome vision. Madame Vestris herself took the part of Oberon and seems thus to have initiated a tradition of contralto fairy kings.

Samuel Phelps's production at the Sadler's Wells Theatre in 1853, with Phelps himself as Bottom, again gave prominence to the moon, first in the forest and then as it shone upon Theseus' palace in Act 5. Charles Kean, at the Princess's Theatre in 1856, gave Puck's opening speech to a nameless fairy in order that the audience might then see Puck (Ellen Terry, aged eight) rising on a mushroom. Kean's set invoked ancient Athens (admittedly not that of Theseus' era) by showing the Acropolis surrounded by marble temples and the theater of Bacchus. A dummy Puck flew through the air to the accompaniment of Mendelssohn's music, and one evening, when the dummy happened to fall to the stage, Ellen Terry got a laugh by going out in view of the audience to pick it up.

The fairies in Augustin Daly's New York production of 1888 flickered like fireflies through the shadowy mists. Frank Benson at the Globe Theatre in London in 1889 similarly had scampering fairies and glittering lights as well as a fight between a spider and a wasp. In 1900, at Her Majesty's Theatre, Herbert Beerbohm Tree provided a carpet of thyme and wildflowers along with the (by now) usual twinkling lights and floating shapes. In 1911 Tree populated his enchanted forest with live rabbits scurrying across the stage of His Majesty's Theatre. In more recent times, Tyrone Guthrie at the Old Vic in London in 1937–1938 concocted a handsome spectacle of dance and moonlit forest, with Vivien Leigh as Titania, Robert Helpmann as Oberon, and Ralph Richardson as Bottom. The tradition of innocent and lavish musical entertainment was fixed on film in Warner Brothers' 1935 *A Midsummer Night's Dream*, directed by Max Reinhardt with a cast that included Dick Powell (Lysander), Olivia de Havilland (Hermia), James Cagney (Bottom), and Mickey Rooney (Puck). The romantic spectacular even included a miniature orchestra of dwarfs performing in the forest. The Shakespeare Memorial Theatre production of 1949, in Stratford-upon-Avon, directed by Michael Benthall, continued the romantic tradition with graceful women in gauze dresses as Titania's fairies.

The other, disillusioning approach to the play dates seemingly from Harley Granville-Barker's interpretation at the Savoy Theatre in London in 1914 on an apron stage in a swift-paced continuous performance, with three symbolic locations (court, forest, town) and a minimum of realistic effects. The costumes suggested something remote, oriental, exotic. Puck made it plain that he was the theatrical manager of affairs onstage; he consciously broke the dramatic illusion, reminding spectators that they were in the theater. From the first, this awareness of the contrivance of theater was an essential part of this new perspective. Harcourt Williams's production at the Old Vic in 1929 (with John Gielgud as Oberon) was a Jacobean masque, its fairies not the gauzy sprites of the Victorians but elemental figures, based on sketches by Inigo Jones, with green faces and costumes of seaweed. George Devine, at the Shakespeare Memorial Theatre in 1954, gave a strange, birdlike aspect to his fairies and an ominous tone to the whole production. Peter Hall, in 1959, directed his young lovers to be foolish and clumsy, devoted to horseplay. Benjamin Britten's striking opera, performed at the Aldeburgh Festival in Suffolk in 1960, invoked a forest full of eerie sounds and disturbing dreamlike effects.

The most influential production in this disillusioning vein is Peter Brook's with the Royal Shakespeare Company in 1970, which was subsequently taken on tour. Plainly acknowledging the influence of Bertolt Brecht, Samuel Beckett, Antonin Artaud, and *Shakespeare Our Contemporary*, by Jan Kott, which argues in an intemperate but insightful way for the darker sexual side of the play, Brook created an intensely self-aware theatrical world within a three-sided brilliantly lit white box. The actors, often on trapezes, were circus performers, athletes, tumblers; Bottom, with his button nose and clumsy shoes, was both ass and circus clown. A fisted arm thrust between his legs as he was carried offstage from his rendezvous with the Fairy Queen suggested a triumphant phallus. The fairies were adult male actors. The production reveled in exposing its stage devices. The actors of Oberon and Titania not only doubled as Theseus and Hippolyta in order to explore a sense in which the fairy king and queen act out the aggressions of their human counterparts, but this doubling was flaunted in the final scene. Oberon and Titania, with a swift change of garments, transformed themselves onstage into Theseus and Hippolyta and were thus able to join the courtly audience of "Pyramus and Thisbe."

Since the time of Brook's pace-setting production, it has not been unusual to see athletic lovers who are unceasingly aggressive toward each other, or fairies who are spaced out on drugs. In 1985, on a bloodred set at the Guthrie Threatre in Minneapolis, Liviu Ciulei produced the play as a dark comedy of sexual strife and patriarchal abuse. The hallmark of modern productions throughout has been the constant use of theatrical illusion as a plaything: Puck and Oberon walk among the mortals, nearly touching them, separated only by the audience's understanding that they are invisible.

Fed by these two acting traditions, Shakespeare's text offers itself for endless speculation and experiment. Certainly the text's own indications for performance encourage the self-conscious methods of presentation that have become so popular in recent productions. Juxtapositions of the seen and unseen run through the play, as when, in Act 2, scene 2, and Act 3, scene 1, Titania sleeps in her bower while first the lovers and then Bottom and company wrestle with love's difficulties or with the problems of rehearsing a play. Possibly her bower was intended for some curtained space backstage in the Elizabethan playhouse, but the full visual contrast is present if she sleeps in view of the audience until she is at length awakened by Bottom's singing. Certainly at the end of Act 4 the four lovers are to remain asleep onstage while Titania first sports with her lover Bottom, then sleeps, and finally is awakened by Oberon; the four lovers are still there when Theseus and his train arrive.

Shakespeare's theater provides ample means, too, of dramatizing the contrasts between court and forest, not (in the original production) through scenery, but by means of costumed actors and their gestures and blocking: Theseus is a figure of noble splendor, richly dressed, accompanied by followers and surrounded by ceremony, while the creatures of the forest visibly come from another world, one of dreams, nighttime, and magic. Whether the fairies are presented benignly, in the romantic tradition of staging, or darkly, through the eyes of disenchantment, the imaginative world they create onstage is one that thrives on tricks of illusion and theatrical self-awareness.

The Playhouse

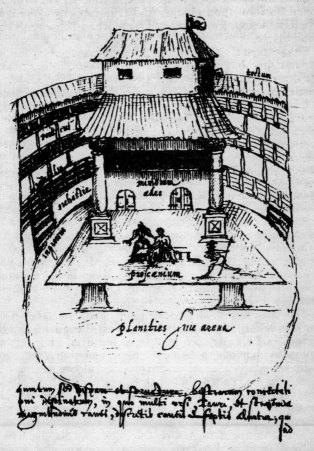

This early copy of a drawing by Johannes de Witt of the Swan Theatre in London (c. 1596), made by his friend Arend van Buchell, is the only surviving contemporary sketch of the interior of a public theater in the 1590s.

From other contemporary evidence, including the stage directions and dialogue of Elizabethan plays, we can surmise that the various public theaters where Shakespeare's plays were produced (the Theatre, the Curtain, the Globe) resembled the Swan in many important particulars, though there must have been some variations as well. The public playhouses were essentially round, or polygonal, and open to the sky, forming an acting arena approximately 70 feet in diameter; they did not have a large curtain with which to open and close a scene, such as we see today in opera and some traditional theater. A platform measuring approximately 43 feet across and 27 feet deep, referred to in the de Witt drawing as the *proscaenium*, projected into the yard, *planities sive arena*. The roof, *tectum*, above the stage and supported by two pillars, could contain machinery for ascents and descents, as were required in several of Shakespeare's late plays. Above this roof was a hut, shown in the drawing with a flag flying atop it and a trumpeter at its door announcing the performance of a play. The underside of the stage roof, called the heavens, was usually richly decorated with symbolic figures of the sun, the moon, and the constellations. The platform stage stood at a height of 5 1/2 feet or so above the yard, providing room under the stage for underworldly effects. A trapdoor, which is not visible in this drawing, gave access to the space below.

The structure at the back of the platform (labeled *mimorum aedes*), known as the tiring-house because it was the actors' attiring (dressing) space, featured at least two doors, as shown here. Some theaters seem to have also had a discovery space, or curtained recessed alcove, perhaps between the two doors—in which Falstaff could have hidden from the sheriff (*1 Henry IV*, 2.4) or Polonius could have eavesdropped on Hamlet and his mother (*Hamlet*, 3.4). This discovery space probably gave the actors a means of access to and from the tiring-house. Curtains may also have been hung in front of the stage doors on occasion. The de Witt drawing shows a gallery above the doors that extends across the back and evidently contains spectators. On occasions when action "above" demanded the use of this space, as when Juliet appears at her "window" (*Romeo and Juliet*, 2.2 and 3.5), the gallery seems to have been used by the actors, but large scenes there were impractical.

The three-tiered auditorium is perhaps best described by Thomas Platter, a visitor to London in 1599 who saw on that occasion Shakespeare's *Julius Caesar* performed at the Globe:

> The playhouses are so constructed that they play on a raised platform, so that everyone has a good view. There are different galleries and places [*orchestra, sedilia, porticus*], however, where the seating is better and more comfortable and therefore more expensive. For whoever cares to stand below only pays one English penny, but if he wishes to sit, he enters by another door [*ingressus*] and pays another penny, while if he desires to sit in the most comfortable seats, which are cushioned, where he not only sees everything well but can also be seen, then he pays yet another English penny at another door. And during the performance food and drink are carried round the audience, so that for what one cares to pay one may also have refreshment.

Scenery was not used, though the theater building itself was handsome enough to invoke a feeling of order and hierarchy that lent itself to the splendor and pageantry onstage. Portable properties, such as thrones, stools, tables, and beds, could be carried or thrust on as needed. In the scene pictured here by de Witt, a lady on a bench, attended perhaps by her waiting-gentlewoman, receives the address of a male figure. If Shakespeare had written *Twelfth Night* by 1596 for performance at the Swan, we could imagine Malvolio appearing like this as he bows before the Countess Olivia and her gentlewoman, Maria.

A
MIDSUMMER
NIGHT'S
DREAM

[*Dramatis Personae*

THESEUS, *Duke of Athens*
HIPPOLYTA, *Queen of the Amazons, betrothed to Theseus*
PHILOSTRATE, *Master of the Revels*
EGEUS, *father of Hermia*

HERMIA, *daughter of Egeus, in love with Lysander*
LYSANDER, *in love with Hermia*
DEMETRIUS, *in love with Hermia and favored by Egeus*
HELENA, *in love with Demetrius*

OBERON, *King of the Fairies*
TITANIA, *Queen of the Fairies*
PUCK, *or* ROBIN GOODFELLOW
PEASEBLOSSOM,
COBWEB,   } *fairies attending*
MOTE,   *Titania*
MUSTARDSEED,
Other FAIRIES *attending*

PETER QUINCE, *a carpenter,*   PROLOGUE
NICK BOTTOM, *a weaver,*   PYRAMUS
FRANCIS FLUTE, *a bellows mender,* } *representing* THISBE
TOM SNOUT, *a tinker,*   WALL
SNUG, *a joiner,*   LION
ROBIN STARVELING, *a tailor,*   MOONSHINE

Lords and Attendants on Theseus and Hippolyta

SCENE: *Athens, and a wood near it*]

1.1 *Enter Theseus, Hippolyta, [and Philostrate,] with others.*

THESEUS
Now, fair Hippolyta, our nuptial hour
Draws on apace. Four happy days bring in
Another moon; but, O, methinks, how slow
This old moon wanes! She lingers my desires,   4
Like to a stepdame or a dowager   5
Long withering out a young man's revenue.   6

HIPPOLYTA
Four days will quickly steep themselves in night,
Four nights will quickly dream away the time;
And then the moon, like to a silver bow
New bent in heaven, shall behold the night
Of our solemnities.

THESEUS   Go, Philostrate,
Stir up the Athenian youth to merriments,
Awake the pert and nimble spirit of mirth,
Turn melancholy forth to funerals;
The pale companion is not for our pomp.   15
                                    [*Exit Philostrate.*]
Hippolyta, I wooed thee with my sword   16
And won thy love doing thee injuries;
But I will wed thee in another key,
With pomp, with triumph, and with reveling.   19

Enter Egeus and his daughter Hermia, and Lysander, and Demetrius.

EGEUS
Happy be Theseus, our renownèd duke!

THESEUS
Thanks, good Egeus. What's the news with thee?

EGEUS
Full of vexation come I, with complaint
Against my child, my daughter Hermia.

1.1. Location: Athens. Theseus' court.
4 lingers postpones, delays the fulfillment of   **5 stepdame** step-
mother.   **dowager** i.e., a widow (whose right of inheritance from her
dead husband is eating into her son's estate)   **6 withering out** causing
to dwindle   **15 companion** fellow.   **pomp** ceremonial magnificence
16 with my sword i.e., in a military engagement against the Amazons,
when Hippolyta was taken captive   **19 triumph** public festivity

Stand forth, Demetrius. My noble lord,
This man hath my consent to marry her.
Stand forth, Lysander. And, my gracious Duke,
This man hath bewitched the bosom of my child.
Thou, thou, Lysander, thou hast given her rhymes
And interchanged love tokens with my child.
Thou hast by moonlight at her window sung
With feigning voice verses of feigning love,   31
And stol'n the impression of her fantasy   32
With bracelets of thy hair, rings, gauds, conceits,   33
Knacks, trifles, nosegays, sweetmeats—messengers   34
Of strong prevailment in unhardened youth.   35
With cunning hast thou filched my daughter's heart,
Turned her obedience, which is due to me,
To stubborn harshness. And, my gracious Duke,
Be it so she will not here before Your Grace   39
Consent to marry with Demetrius,
I beg the ancient privilege of Athens:
As she is mine, I may dispose of her,
Which shall be either to this gentleman
Or to her death, according to our law
Immediately provided in that case.   45

THESEUS
What say you, Hermia? Be advised, fair maid.
To you your father should be as a god—
One that composed your beauties, yea, and one
To whom you are but as a form in wax
By him imprinted, and within his power
To leave the figure or disfigure it.   51
Demetrius is a worthy gentleman.

HERMIA
So is Lysander.

THESEUS   In himself he is;
But in this kind, wanting your father's voice,   54
The other must be held the worthier.

---

31 feigning (1) counterfeiting (2) faining, desirous   **32 And . . . fantasy**
and made her fall in love with you (imprinting your image on her
imagination) by stealthy and dishonest means   **33 gauds** playthings.
conceits fanciful trifles   **34 Knacks** knickknacks   **35 prevailment in**
influence on   **39 Be it so** if   **45 Immediately** directly, with nothing
intervening   **51 leave** i.e., leave unaltered.   **disfigure** obliterate
54 kind respect.   **wanting** lacking.   **voice** approval

HERMIA
I would my father looked but with my eyes.

THESEUS
Rather your eyes must with his judgment look.

HERMIA
I do entreat Your Grace to pardon me.
I know not by what power I am made bold,
Nor how it may concern my modesty   60
In such a presence here to plead my thoughts;
But I beseech Your Grace that I may know
The worst that may befall me in this case
If I refuse to wed Demetrius.

THESEUS
Either to die the death or to abjure
Forever the society of men.
Therefore, fair Hermia, question your desires,
Know of your youth, examine well your blood,   68
Whether, if you yield not to your father's choice,
You can endure the livery of a nun,   70
For aye to be in shady cloister mewed,   71
To live a barren sister all your life,
Chanting faint hymns to the cold fruitless moon.
Thrice blessèd they that master so their blood
To undergo such maiden pilgrimage;
But earthlier happy is the rose distilled   76
Than that which, withering on the virgin thorn,
Grows, lives, and dies in single blessedness.

HERMIA
So will I grow, so live, so die, my lord,
Ere I will yield my virgin patent up   80
Unto his lordship, whose unwishèd yoke
My soul consents not to give sovereignty.

THESEUS
Take time to pause, and by the next new moon—
The sealing day betwixt my love and me
For everlasting bond of fellowship—
Upon that day either prepare to die
For disobedience to your father's will,
Or else to wed Demetrius, as he would,   88

60 concern befit   **68 blood** passions   **70 livery** habit   **71 aye** ever.
mewed shut in. (Said of a hawk, poultry, etc.)   **76 earthlier happy**
happier as respects this world   **80 patent** privilege   **88 Or** either

Or on Diana's altar to protest   89
For aye austerity and single life.

DEMETRIUS
Relent, sweet Hermia, and, Lysander, yield
Thy crazèd title to my certain right.   92

LYSANDER
You have her father's love, Demetrius;
Let me have Hermia's. Do you marry him.

EGEUS
Scornful Lysander! True, he hath my love,
And what is mine my love shall render him.
And she is mine, and all my right of her
I do estate unto Demetrius.   98

LYSANDER
I am, my lord, as well derived as he,   99
As well possessed; my love is more than his;   100
My fortunes every way as fairly ranked,   101
If not with vantage, as Demetrius';   102
And, which is more than all these boasts can be,
I am beloved of beauteous Hermia.
Why should not I then prosecute my right?
Demetrius, I'll avouch it to his head,   106
Made love to Nedar's daughter, Helena,
And won her soul; and she, sweet lady, dotes,
Devoutly dotes, dotes in idolatry,
Upon this spotted and inconstant man.   110

THESEUS
I must confess that I have heard so much,
And with Demetrius thought to have spoke thereof;
But, being overfull of self-affairs,   113
My mind did lose it. But, Demetrius, come,
And come, Egeus, you shall go with me;
I have some private schooling for you both.   116
For you, fair Hermia, look you arm yourself   117
To fit your fancies to your father's will;   118

89 protest vow   **92 crazèd** cracked, unsound   **98 estate unto** settle or
bestow upon   **99 derived** descended, i.e., as well born   **100 possessed**
endowed with wealth   **101 fairly** handsomely   **102 vantage** superior-
ity   **106 head** i.e., face   **110 spotted** i.e., morally stained   **113 self-
affairs** my own concerns   **116 schooling** admonition   **117 look you arm**
take care you prepare   **118 fancies** likings, thoughts of love

Or else the law of Athens yields you up—
Which by no means we may extenuate—   120
To death or to a vow of single life.
Come, my Hippolyta. What cheer, my love?
Demetrius and Egeus, go along.   123
I must employ you in some business
Against our nuptial and confer with you   125
Of something nearly that concerns yourselves.   126

EGEUS
With duty and desire we follow you.
                    Exeunt [all but Lysander and Hermia].

LYSANDER
How now, my love, why is your cheek so pale?
How chance the roses there do fade so fast?

HERMIA
Belike for want of rain, which I could well   130
Beteem them from the tempest of my eyes.   131

LYSANDER
Ay me! For aught that I could ever read,
Could ever hear by tale or history,
The course of true love never did run smooth;
But either it was different in blood—   135

HERMIA
O cross! Too high to be enthralled to low.   136

LYSANDER
Or else misgrafted in respect of years—   137

HERMIA
O spite! Too old to be engaged to young.

LYSANDER
Or else it stood upon the choice of friends—   139

HERMIA
O hell, to choose love by another's eyes!

LYSANDER
Or if there were a sympathy in choice,   141
War, death, or sickness did lay siege to it,
Making it momentany as a sound,   143

120 extenuate mitigate   **123 go** i.e., come   **125 Against** in preparation
for   **126 nearly that** that closely   **130 Belike** very likely   **131 Beteem**
grant, afford   **135 blood** hereditary station   **136 cross** vexation
137 misgrafted ill grafted, badly matched   **139 friends** relatives
141 sympathy agreement   **143 momentany** lasting but a moment

Swift as a shadow, short as any dream,
Brief as the lightning in the collied night,   145
That in a spleen unfolds both heaven and earth,   146
And ere a man hath power to say "Behold!"
The jaws of darkness do devour it up.
So quick bright things come to confusion.   149

HERMIA
If then true lovers have been ever crossed,   150
It stands as an edict in destiny.
Then let us teach our trial patience,   152
Because it is a customary cross,
As due to love as thoughts and dreams and sighs,
Wishes and tears, poor fancy's followers.   155

LYSANDER
A good persuasion. Therefore, hear me, Hermia: 156
I have a widow aunt, a dowager
Of great revenue, and she hath no child.
From Athens is her house remote seven leagues;
And she respects me as her only son.   160
There, gentle Hermia, may I marry thee,
And to that place the sharp Athenian law
Cannot pursue us. If thou lovest me, then,
Steal forth thy father's house tomorrow night;
And in the wood, a league without the town,
Where I did meet thee once with Helena
To do observance to a morn of May,   167
There will I stay for thee.

HERMIA   My good Lysander!
I swear to thee by Cupid's strongest bow,
By his best arrow with the golden head,   170
By the simplicity of Venus' doves,   171
By that which knitteth souls and prospers loves,

---

145 collied blackened (as with coal dust), darkened   **146 in a spleen** in a
swift impulse, in a violent flash.   **unfolds** discloses   **149 quick** quickly;
or, perhaps, living, alive.   **confusion** ruin   **150 ever crossed** always
thwarted   **152 teach . . . patience** i.e., teach ourselves patience in this
trial   **155 fancy's** amorous passion's   **156 persuasion** conviction
160 respects regards   **167 do . . . May** perform the ceremonies of May
Day   **170 best arrow** (Cupid's best gold-pointed arrows were supposed
to induce love, his blunt leaden arrows, aversion.)   **171 simplicity** innocence.   **doves** i.e., those that drew Venus' chariot

And by that fire which burned the Carthage queen   173
When the false Trojan under sail was seen,   174
By all the vows that ever men have broke,
In number more than ever women spoke,
In that same place thou hast appointed me
Tomorrow truly will I meet with thee.

LYSANDER
Keep promise, love. Look, here comes Helena.

Enter Helena.

HERMIA
God speed, fair Helena! Whither away?   180

HELENA
Call you me fair? That "fair" again unsay.
Demetrius loves your fair. O happy fair!   182
Your eyes are lodestars, and your tongue's sweet air   183
More tunable than lark to shepherd's ear   184
When wheat is green, when hawthorn buds appear.
Sickness is catching. O, were favor so!   186
Yours would I catch, fair Hermia, ere I go;
My ear should catch your voice, my eye your eye,
My tongue should catch your tongue's sweet melody.
Were the world mine, Demetrius being bated,   190
The rest I'd give to be to you translated.   191
O, teach me how you look and with what art
You sway the motion of Demetrius' heart.   193

HERMIA
I frown upon him, yet he loves me still.

HELENA
O, that your frowns would teach my smiles such skill!

HERMIA
I give him curses, yet he gives me love.

HELENA
O, that my prayers could such affection move!   197

173, 174 Carthage queen, false Trojan (Dido, Queen of Carthage, immo-
lated herself on a funeral pyre after having been deserted by the Trojan
hero Aeneas.) **180 fair** fair-complexioned (generally regarded by the
Elizabethans as more beautiful than dark complexion) **182 your fair**
your beauty (even though Hermia is dark-complexioned). **happy fair**
lucky fair one **183 lodestars** guiding stars. **air** music **184 tunable**
tuneful, melodious **186 favor** appearance, looks **190 bated** excepted
191 translated transformed **193 motion** impulse **197 affection** passion. **move** arouse

HERMIA
  The more I hate, the more he follows me.

HELENA
  The more I love, the more he hateth me.

HERMIA
  His folly, Helena, is no fault of mine.

HELENA
  None but your beauty. Would that fault were mine!

HERMIA
  Take comfort. He no more shall see my face.
  Lysander and myself will fly this place.
  Before the time I did Lysander see
  Seemed Athens as a paradise to me.
  O, then, what graces in my love do dwell
  That he hath turned a heaven unto a hell!

LYSANDER
  Helen, to you our minds we will unfold.
  Tomorrow night, when Phoebe doth behold   209
  Her silver visage in the watery glass,   210
  Decking with liquid pearl the bladed grass,
  A time that lovers' flights doth still conceal,   212
  Through Athens' gates have we devised to steal.

HERMIA
  And in the wood, where often you and I
  Upon faint primrose beds were wont to lie,   215
  Emptying our bosoms of their counsel sweet,   216
  There my Lysander and myself shall meet;
  And thence from Athens turn away our eyes,
  To seek new friends and stranger companies.
  Farewell, sweet playfellow. Pray thou for us,
  And good luck grant thee thy Demetrius!
  Keep word, Lysander. We must starve our sight
  From lovers' food till morrow deep midnight.

LYSANDER
  I will, my Hermia.   *Exit Hermia.*
              Helena, adieu.
  As you on him, Demetrius dote on you!
                                              Exit Lysander.

209 Phoebe Diana, the moon   **210 glass** mirror   **212 still** always
215 faint pale   **216 counsel** secret thought

HELENA

How happy some o'er other some can be!   226
Through Athens I am thought as fair as she.
But what of that? Demetrius thinks not so;
He will not know what all but he do know.
And as he errs, doting on Hermia's eyes,
So I, admiring of his qualities.   231
Things base and vile, holding no quantity,   232
Love can transpose to form and dignity.
Love looks not with the eyes, but with the mind,
And therefore is winged Cupid painted blind.
Nor hath Love's mind of any judgment taste;   236
Wings, and no eyes, figure unheedy haste.   237
And therefore is Love said to be a child,
Because in choice he is so oft beguiled.
As waggish boys in game themselves forswear,   240
So the boy Love is perjured everywhere.
For ere Demetrius looked on Hermia's eyne,   242
He hailed down oaths that he was only mine;
And when this hail some heat from Hermia felt,
So he dissolved, and showers of oaths did melt.
I will go tell him of fair Hermia's flight.
Then to the wood will he tomorrow night
Pursue her; and for this intelligence   248
If I have thanks, it is a dear expense.   249
But herein mean I to enrich my pain,
To have his sight thither and back again.   *Exit.*

❖

1.2   *Enter Quince the carpenter, and Snug the
joiner, and Bottom the weaver, and Flute the
bellows mender, and Snout the tinker, and
Starveling the tailor.*

---

226 o'er . . . can be can be in comparison to some others   **231 admiring
of** wondering at   **232 holding no quantity** i.e., unsubstantial, unshapely
236 Nor . . . taste i.e., nor has Love, which dwells in the fancy or
imagination, any *taste* or least bit of judgment or reason   **237 figure**
are a symbol of   **240 waggish** playful, mischievous.   **game** sport, jest
242 eyne eyes. (Old form of plural.)   **248 intelligence** information   **249 a
dear expense** i.e., a trouble worth taking.   **dear** costly

1.2. Location: Athens.

QUINCE   Is all our company here?

BOTTOM   You were best to call them generally, man by
man, according to the scrip.

QUINCE   Here is the scroll of every man's name which is
thought fit, through all Athens, to play in our interlude
before the Duke and the Duchess on his wedding day
at night.

BOTTOM   First, good Peter Quince, say what the play
treats on, then read the names of the actors, and so
grow to a point.

QUINCE   Marry, our play is "The most lamentable comedy and most cruel death of Pyramus and Thisbe."

BOTTOM   A very good piece of work, I assure you, and
a merry. Now, good Peter Quince, call forth your actors by the scroll. Masters, spread yourselves.

QUINCE   Answer as I call you. Nick Bottom, the weaver.

BOTTOM   Ready. Name what part I am for, and proceed.

QUINCE   You, Nick Bottom, are set down for Pyramus.

BOTTOM   What is Pyramus? A lover or a tyrant?

QUINCE   A lover, that kills himself most gallant for love.

BOTTOM   That will ask some tears in the true performing
of it. If I do it, let the audience look to their eyes. I will
move storms; I will condole in some measure. To the
rest—yet my chief humor is for a tyrant. I could play
Ercles rarely, or a part to tear a cat in, to make all split.

> "The raging rocks
> And shivering shocks
> Shall break the locks
>   Of prison gates;
> And Phibbus' car
> Shall shine from far
> And make and mar
>   The foolish Fates."

This was lofty! Now name the rest of the players. This is

Line numbers: 2, 3, 10, 11, 16, 23, 24, 25, 30

---

2 generally (Bottom's blunder for *individually*.)   **3 scrip** scrap. (Bottom's error for *script*.)   **10 grow to** come to   **11 Marry** (A mild oath,
originally the name of the Virgin Mary.)   **16 Bottom** (As a weaver's
term, a *bottom* was an object around which thread was wound.)
23 condole lament, arouse pity   **24 humor** inclination, whim   **25 Ercles**
Hercules. (The tradition of ranting came from Seneca's *Hercules
Furens*.)   **tear a cat** i.e., rant.   **make all split** i.e., cause a stir, bring the
house down   **30 Phibbus' car** Phoebus', the sun-god's, chariot

Ercles' vein, a tyrant's vein. A lover is more condoling.

QUINCE   Francis Flute, the bellows mender.

FLUTE   Here, Peter Quince.

QUINCE   Flute, you must take Thisbe on you.

FLUTE   What is Thisbe? A wandering knight?

QUINCE   It is the lady that Pyramus must love.

FLUTE   Nay, faith, let not me play a woman. I have a
beard coming.

QUINCE   That's all one. You shall play it in a mask, and   43
you may speak as small as you will.   44

BOTTOM   An I may hide my face, let me play Thisbe too.   45
I'll speak in a monstrous little voice, "Thisne, Thisne!"
"Ah Pyramus, my lover dear! Thy Thisbe dear, and
lady dear!"

QUINCE   No, no, you must play Pyramus, and, Flute,
you Thisbe.

BOTTOM   Well, proceed.

QUINCE   Robin Starveling, the tailor.

STARVELING   Here, Peter Quince.

QUINCE   Robin Starveling, you must play Thisbe's
mother. Tom Snout, the tinker.

SNOUT   Here, Peter Quince.

QUINCE   You, Pyramus' father; myself, Thisbe's father;
Snug, the joiner, you, the lion's part; and I hope here
is a play fitted.

SNUG   Have you the lion's part written? Pray you, if it
be, give it me, for I am slow of study.

QUINCE   You may do it extempore, for it is nothing but
roaring.

BOTTOM   Let me play the lion too. I will roar that I will
do any man's heart good to hear me. I will roar that I
will make the Duke say, "Let him roar again, let him
roar again."

QUINCE   An you should do it too terribly, you would
fright the Duchess and the ladies, that they would
shriek; and that were enough to hang us all.

ALL   That would hang us, every mother's son.

BOTTOM   I grant you, friends, if you should fright the

---

43 That's all one it makes no difference   **44 small** high-pitched   **45 An**
if (also at l. 68)

ladies out of their wits, they would have no more discretion but to hang us; but I will aggravate my voice 74
so that I will roar you as gently as any sucking dove; I 75
will roar you an 'twere any nightingale.

QUINCE   You can play no part but Pyramus; for Pyramus
is a sweet-faced man, a proper man as one shall see in 78
a summer's day, a most lovely gentlemanlike man.
Therefore you must needs play Pyramus.

BOTTOM   Well, I will undertake it. What beard were I
best to play it in?

QUINCE   Why, what you will.

BOTTOM   I will discharge it in either your straw-color 84
beard, your orange-tawny beard, your purple-in-grain 85
beard, or your French-crown-color beard, your perfect 86
yellow.

QUINCE   Some of your French crowns have no hair at all, 88
and then you will play barefaced. But, masters, here
are your parts. [*He distributes parts.*] And I am to entreat you, request you, and desire you to con them by 91
tomorrow night; and meet me in the palace wood, a
mile without the town, by moonlight. There will we
rehearse; for if we meet in the city, we shall be dogged
with company, and our devices known. In the mean- 95
time I will draw a bill of properties, such as our play 96
wants. I pray you, fail me not.

BOTTOM   We will meet, and there we may rehearse most
obscenely and courageously. Take pains, be perfect; 99
adieu.

QUINCE   At the Duke's oak we meet.

BOTTOM   Enough. Hold, or cut bowstrings.   *Exeunt.* 102

❖

74 aggravate (Bottom's blunder for *moderate*.)   **75 roar you** i.e., roar for
you.   **sucking dove** (Bottom conflates *sitting dove* and *sucking lamb*,
two proverbial images of innocence.)   **78 proper** handsome   **84 discharge** perform.   **your** i.e., you know the kind I mean   **85 purple-in-
grain** dyed a very deep red. (From *grain*, the name applied to the dried
insect used to make the dye.)   **86 French-crown-color** i.e., color of a
French crown, a gold coin   **88 crowns** heads bald from syphilis, the
"French disease"   **91 con** learn by heart   **95 devices** plans   **96 bill**
list   **99 obscenely** (An unintentionally funny blunder, whatever Bottom
meant to say.)   **perfect** i.e., letter-perfect in memorizing your parts
102 Hold . . . bowstrings (An archers' expression not definitely explained,
but probably meaning here "keep your promises, or give up the play.")

2.1   *Enter a Fairy at one door, and Robin*
         Goodfellow [Puck] at another.

PUCK
  How now, spirit, whither wander you?
FAIRY
          Over hill, over dale,
            Thorough bush, thorough brier,   3
          Over park, over pale,   4
            Thorough flood, thorough fire,
          I do wander everywhere,
          Swifter than the moon's sphere;   7
          And I serve the Fairy Queen,
          To dew her orbs upon the green.   9
          The cowslips tall her pensioners be.   10
          In their gold coats spots you see:
          Those be rubies, fairy favors;   12
          In those freckles live their savors.   13
  I must go seek some dewdrops here
  And hang a pearl in every cowslip's ear.
  Farewell, thou lob of spirits; I'll be gone.   16
  Our Queen and all her elves come here anon.   17
PUCK
  The King doth keep his revels here tonight.
  Take heed the Queen come not within his sight.
  For Oberon is passing fell and wrath,   20
  Because that she as her attendant hath
  A lovely boy, stolen from an Indian king;
  She never had so sweet a changeling.   23
  And jealous Oberon would have the child
  Knight of his train, to trace the forests wild.   25
  But she perforce withholds the lovèd boy,   26
  Crowns him with flowers, and makes him all her joy.

2.1. Location: A wood near Athens.
3 Thorough through   **4 pale** enclosure   **7 sphere** orbit   **9 orbs** circles,
i.e., fairy rings (circular bands of grass, darker than the surrounding
area, caused by fungi enriching the soil)   **10 pensioners** retainers,
members of the royal bodyguard   **12 favors** love tokens   **13 savors**
sweet smells   **16 lob** country bumpkin   **17 anon** at once   **20 passing
fell** exceedingly angry.   **wrath** wrathful   **23 changeling** child exchanged
for another by the fairies   **25 trace** range through   **26 perforce** forcibly

And now they never meet in grove or green,
By fountain clear, or spangled starlight sheen,   29
But they do square, that all their elves for fear   30
Creep into acorn cups and hide them there.

FAIRY

Either I mistake your shape and making quite,
Or else you are that shrewd and knavish sprite   33
Called Robin Goodfellow. Are not you he
That frights the maidens of the villagery,   35
Skim milk, and sometimes labor in the quern,   36
And bootless make the breathless huswife churn,   37
And sometimes make the drink to bear no barm,   38
Mislead night wanderers, laughing at their harm?
Those that "Hobgoblin" call you, and "Sweet Puck,"
You do their work, and they shall have good luck.
Are you not he?

PUCK   Thou speakest aright;
I am that merry wanderer of the night.
I jest to Oberon and make him smile
When I a fat and bean-fed horse beguile,
Neighing in likeness of a filly foal;
And sometimes lurk I in a gossip's bowl,   47
In very likeness of a roasted crab,   48
And when she drinks, against her lips I bob
And on her withered dewlap pour the ale.   50
The wisest aunt, telling the saddest tale,   51
Sometimes for three-foot stool mistaketh me;
Then slip I from her bum, down topples she,
And "Tailor" cries, and falls into a cough;   54
And then the whole choir hold their hips and laugh,   55
And waxen in their mirth, and neeze, and swear   56
A merrier hour was never wasted there.
But, room, fairy! Here comes Oberon.   58

FAIRY

And here my mistress. Would that he were gone!

29 fountain spring. **starlight sheen** shining starlight   **30 square** quarrel **33 shrewd** mischievous. **sprite** spirit   **35 villagery** village popula-
tion **36 quern** handmill **37 bootless** in vain. **huswife** housewife
38 barm yeast, head on the ale   **47 gossip's** old woman's   **48 crab** crab
apple **50 dewlap** loose skin on neck **51 aunt** old woman. **saddest**
most serious **54 Tailor** (Possibly because she ends up sitting cross-
legged on the floor, looking like a tailor.) **55 choir** company **56 waxen**
increase. **neeze** sneeze **58 room** stand aside, make room

Enter [Oberon] the King of Fairies at one door,
with his train; and [Titania] the Queen at
another, with hers.

OBERON
  Ill met by moonlight, proud Titania.

TITANIA
  What, jealous Oberon? Fairies, skip hence.
  I have forsworn his bed and company.

OBERON
  Tarry, rash wanton. Am not I thy lord?   63

TITANIA
  Then I must be thy lady; but I know
  When thou hast stolen away from Fairyland
  And in the shape of Corin sat all day,   66
  Playing on pipes of corn and versing love   67
  To amorous Phillida. Why art thou here   68
  Come from the farthest step of India   69
  But that, forsooth, the bouncing Amazon,
  Your buskined mistress and your warrior love,   71
  To Theseus must be wedded, and you come
  To give their bed joy and prosperity.

OBERON
  How canst thou thus for shame, Titania,
  Glance at my credit with Hippolyta,   75
  Knowing I know thy love to Theseus?
  Didst not thou lead him through the glimmering night
  From Perigenia, whom he ravishèd?   78
  And make him with fair Aegles break his faith,   79
  With Ariadne and Antiopa?   80

63 wanton headstrong creature   **66, 68 Corin, Phillida** (Conventional names of pastoral lovers.)   **67 corn** (Here, oat stalks.)
69 step farthest limit of travel, or, perhaps, *steep*, mountain range
71 buskined wearing half-boots called buskins   **75 Glance . . .
Hippolyta** make insinuations about my favored relationship with
Hippolyta   **78 Perigenia** i.e., Perigouna, one of Theseus' conquests.
(This and the following women are named in Thomas North's translation
of Plutarch's "Life of Theseus.")   **79 Aegles** i.e., Aegle, for whom
Theseus deserted Ariadne according to some accounts   **80 Ariadne**
the daughter of Minos, King of Crete, who helped Theseus to escape
the labyrinth after killing the Minotaur; later she was abandoned
by Theseus.   **Antiopa** Queen of the Amazons and wife of Theseus;
elsewhere identified with Hippolyta, but here thought of as a separate
woman

TITANIA
These are the forgeries of jealousy;
And never, since the middle summer's spring,   82
Met we on hill, in dale, forest, or mead,
By pavèd fountain or by rushy brook,   84
Or in the beachèd margent of the sea,   85
To dance our ringlets to the whistling wind,   86
But with thy brawls thou hast disturbed our sport.
Therefore the winds, piping to us in vain,
As in revenge, have sucked up from the sea
Contagious fogs; which, falling in the land,   90
Hath every pelting river made so proud   91
That they have overborne their continents.   92
The ox hath therefore stretched his yoke in vain,
The plowman lost his sweat, and the green corn   94
Hath rotted ere his youth attained a beard;
The fold stands empty in the drownèd field,   96
And crows are fatted with the murrain flock;   97
The nine-men's-morris is filled up with mud,   98
And the quaint mazes in the wanton green   99
For lack of tread are undistinguishable.
The human mortals want their winter here;   101
No night is now with hymn or carol blessed.
Therefore the moon, the governess of floods,   103
Pale in her anger, washes all the air,
That rheumatic diseases do abound.   105
And thorough this distemperature we see   106
The seasons alter: hoary-headed frosts
Fall in the fresh lap of the crimson rose,
And on old Hiems' thin and icy crown   109

82 middle summer's spring beginning of midsummer **84 pavèd** with
pebbled bottom. **rushy** bordered with rushes **85 in** on. **margent**
edge, border **86 ringlets** dances in a ring. (See *orbs* in l. 9.) **90 Contagious** noxious **91 pelting** paltry **92 continents** banks that contain
them **94 corn** grain of any kind **96 fold** pen for sheep or cattle
97 murrain having died of the plague **98 nine-men's-morris** i.e., portion of the village green marked out in a square for a game played with
nine pebbles or pegs **99 quaint mazes** i.e., intricate paths marked out
on the village green to be followed rapidly on foot as a kind of con-
test. **wanton** luxuriant **101 want** lack. **winter** i.e., regular winter
season; or, proper observances of winter, such as the *hymn or carol* in
the next line (?) **103 Therefore** i.e., as a result of our quarrel
105 rheumatic diseases colds, flu, and other respiratory infections
106 distemperature disturbance in nature **109 Hiems'** the winter god's

An odorous chaplet of sweet summer buds
Is, as in mockery, set. The spring, the summer,
The childing autumn, angry winter, change   112
Their wonted liveries, and the mazèd world   113
By their increase now knows not which is which.   114
And this same progeny of evils comes
From our debate, from our dissension;   116
We are their parents and original.   117

OBERON
Do you amend it, then; it lies in you.
Why should Titania cross her Oberon?
I do but beg a little changeling boy
To be my henchman.

TITANIA   Set your heart at rest.   121
The fairy land buys not the child of me.
His mother was a vot'ress of my order,
And in the spicèd Indian air by night
Full often hath she gossiped by my side
And sat with me on Neptune's yellow sands,
Marking th' embarkèd traders on the flood,   127
When we have laughed to see the sails conceive
And grow big-bellied with the wanton wind;   129
Which she, with pretty and with swimming gait,   130
Following—her womb then rich with my young squire—
Would imitate, and sail upon the land
To fetch me trifles, and return again
As from a voyage, rich with merchandise.
But she, being mortal, of that boy did die;
And for her sake do I rear up her boy,
And for her sake I will not part with him.

OBERON
How long within this wood intend you stay?

TITANIA
Perchance till after Theseus' wedding day.
If you will patiently dance in our round   140
And see our moonlight revels, go with us;

112 childing fruitful, pregnant   113 wonted liveries usual apparel.
mazèd bewildered   114 their increase their yield, what they produce
116 debate quarrel   117 original origin   121 henchman attendant,
page   127 traders trading vessels.   flood flood tide   129 wanton
sportive   130 swimming smooth, gliding   140 round circular
dance

If not, shun me, and I will spare your haunts.   142

OBERON
Give me that boy and I will go with thee.

TITANIA
Not for thy fairy kingdom. Fairies, away!
We shall chide downright if I longer stay.
                    Exeunt [Titania with her train].

OBERON
Well, go thy way. Thou shalt not from this grove   146
Till I torment thee for this injury.
My gentle Puck, come hither. Thou rememb'rest
Since once I sat upon a promontory,   149
And heard a mermaid on a dolphin's back
Uttering such dulcet and harmonious breath   151
That the rude sea grew civil at her song,   152
And certain stars shot madly from their spheres
To hear the sea-maid's music.
PUCK   I remember.
OBERON
That very time I saw, but thou couldst not,
Flying between the cold moon and the earth,
Cupid all armed. A certain aim he took   157
At a fair vestal thronèd by the west,   158
And loosed his love shaft smartly from his bow   159
As it should pierce a hundred thousand hearts;   160
But I might see young Cupid's fiery shaft   161
Quenched in the chaste beams of the watery moon,
And the imperial vot'ress passèd on
In maiden meditation, fancy-free.   164
Yet marked I where the bolt of Cupid fell: 165
It fell upon a little western flower,
Before milk-white, now purple with love's wound,
And maidens call it "love-in-idleness."   168
Fetch me that flower; the herb I showed thee once.
The juice of it on sleeping eyelids laid

142 **spare** shun   146 **from** go from   149 **Since** when   151 **breath** voice,
song   152 **rude** rough   157 **all** fully   158 **vestal** vestal virgin. (Contains
a complimentary allusion to Queen Elizabeth as a votaress of Diana and
probably refers to an actual entertainment in her honor at Elvetham in
1591.)   159 **loosed** released   160 **As** as if   161 **might** could   164 **fancy-
free** free of love's spell   165 **bolt** arrow   168 **love-in-idleness** pansy,
heartsease

Will make or man or woman madly dote   171
Upon the next live creature that it sees.
Fetch me this herb, and be thou here again
Ere the leviathan can swim a league.   174

PUCK
I'll put a girdle round about the earth
In forty minutes.   [*Exit.*]
OBERON   Having once this juice,   176
I'll watch Titania when she is asleep
And drop the liquor of it in her eyes.
The next thing then she waking looks upon,
Be it on lion, bear, or wolf, or bull,
On meddling monkey, or on busy ape,
She shall pursue it with the soul of love.
And ere I take this charm from off her sight,
As I can take it with another herb,
I'll make her render up her page to me.
But who comes here? I am invisible,
And I will overhear their conference.

Enter Demetrius. Helena following him.

DEMETRIUS
I love thee not; therefore pursue me not.
Where is Lysander and fair Hermia?
The one I'll slay; the other slayeth me.
Thou toldst me they were stol'n unto this wood;
And here am I, and wode within this wood,   192
Because I cannot meet my Hermia.
Hence, get thee gone, and follow me no more.

HELENA
You draw me, you hardhearted adamant!   195
But yet you draw not iron, for my heart
Is true as steel. Leave you your power to draw,   197
And I shall have no power to follow you.

DEMETRIUS
Do I entice you? Do I speak you fair?   199

---

171 or . . . or either . . . or **174 leviathan** sea monster, whale **176 forty**
(Used indefinitely.) **192 wode** mad. (Pronounced "wood" and often
spelled so.) **195 adamant** lodestone, magnet (with pun on *hardhearted*,
since adamant was also thought to be the hardest of all stones and was
confused with the diamond) **197 Leave** give up **199 fair** courteously

Or rather do I not in plainest truth
Tell you I do not nor I cannot love you?

HELENA

And even for that do I love you the more.
I am your spaniel; and, Demetrius,
The more you beat me, I will fawn on you.
Use me but as your spaniel, spurn me, strike me,
Neglect me, lose me; only give me leave,
Unworthy as I am, to follow you.
What worser place can I beg in your love—
And yet a place of high respect with me—
Than to be used as you use your dog?

DEMETRIUS

Tempt not too much the hatred of my spirit,
For I am sick when I do look on thee.

HELENA

And I am sick when I look not on you.

DEMETRIUS

You do impeach your modesty too much   214
To leave the city and commit yourself
Into the hands of one that loves you not,
To trust the opportunity of night
And the ill counsel of a desert place   218
With the rich worth of your virginity.

HELENA

Your virtue is my privilege. For that   220
It is not night when I do see your face,
Therefore I think I am not in the night;
Nor doth this wood lack worlds of company,
For you, in my respect, are all the world.   224
Then how can it be said I am alone
When all the world is here to look on me?

DEMETRIUS

I'll run from thee and hide me in the brakes,   227
And leave thee to the mercy of wild beasts.

HELENA

The wildest hath not such a heart as you.
Run when you will, the story shall be changed:

214 impeach call into question   **218 desert** deserted   **220 virtue** good-
ness or power to attract.   **privilege** safeguard, warrant.   **For that**
because   **224 in my respect** as far as I am concerned   **227 brakes**
thickets

Apollo flies and Daphne holds the chase,   231
The dove pursues the griffin, the mild hind   232
Makes speed to catch the tiger—bootless speed,   233
When cowardice pursues and valor flies!

DEMETRIUS
I will not stay thy questions. Let me go!   235
Or if thou follow me, do not believe
But I shall do thee mischief in the wood.

HELENA
Ay, in the temple, in the town, the field,
You do me mischief. Fie, Demetrius!
Your wrongs do set a scandal on my sex.   240
We cannot fight for love, as men may do;
We should be wooed and were not made to woo.
                              [Exit Demetrius.]
I'll follow thee and make a heaven of hell,
To die upon the hand I love so well.   *[Exit.]* 244

OBERON
Fare thee well, nymph. Ere he do leave this grove,
Thou shalt fly him and he shall seek thy love.

        Enter Puck.

Hast thou the flower there? Welcome, wanderer.

PUCK
Ay, there it is.   '   *[He offers the flower.]*

OBERON   I pray thee, give it me.
I know a bank where the wild thyme blows,   249
Where oxlips and the nodding violet grows,   250
Quite overcanopied with luscious woodbine,   251
With sweet muskroses and with eglantine.   252
There sleeps Titania sometimes of the night,
Lulled in these flowers with dances and delight;

---

231 Apollo . . . chase (In the ancient myth, Daphne fled from Apollo and
was saved from rape by being transformed into a laurel tree; here it is
the female who *holds the chase*, or pursues, instead of the male.)
232 griffin a fabulous monster with the head of an eagle and the body
of a lion. **hind** female deer **233 bootless** fruitless **235 stay** wait
for. **questions** talk or argument **240 Your . . . sex** i.e., the wrongs
that you do me cause me to act in a manner that disgraces my sex
244 upon by **249 blows** blooms **250 oxlips** flowers resembling cowslip
and primrose **251 woodbine** honeysuckle **252 muskroses** a kind of
large, sweet-scented rose. **eglantine** sweetbrier, another kind of rose

And there the snake throws her enameled skin,   255
Weed wide enough to wrap a fairy in.   256
And with the juice of this I'll streak her eyes   257
And make her full of hateful fantasies.
Take thou some of it, and seek through this grove.
                    [*He gives some love juice.*]
A sweet Athenian lady is in love
With a disdainful youth. Anoint his eyes,
But do it when the next thing he espies
May be the lady. Thou shalt know the man
By the Athenian garments he hath on.
Effect it with some care, that he may prove
More fond on her than she upon her love;   266
And look thou meet me ere the first cock crow.

PUCK
Fear not, my lord, your servant shall do so.
                                Exeunt.

❖

2.2   *Enter Titania, Queen of Fairies, with her train.*

TITANIA
Come, now a roundel and a fairy song;   1
Then, for the third part of a minute, hence—
Some to kill cankers in the muskrose buds,   3
Some war with reremice for their leathern wings   4
To make my small elves coats, and some keep back
The clamorous owl, that nightly hoots and wonders
At our quaint spirits. Sing me now asleep.   7
Then to your offices, and let me rest.

    Fairies sing.

FIRST FAIRY
    You spotted snakes with double tongue,   9
        Thorny hedgehogs, be not seen;

---

255 throws sloughs off, sheds   **256 Weed** garment   **257 streak** anoint, touch gently   **266 fond on** doting on

2.2. Location: The wood.
1 roundel dance in a ring   **3 cankers** cankerworms (i.e., caterpillars or grubs)   **4 reremice** bats   **7 quaint** dainty   **9 double** forked

Newts and blindworms, do no wrong,   11
   Come not near our Fairy Queen.

CHORUS

   Philomel, with melody   13
   Sing in our sweet lullaby;
Lulla, lulla, lullaby, lulla, lulla, lullaby.
    Never harm
    Nor spell nor charm
  Come our lovely lady nigh.
  So good night, with lullaby.

FIRST FAIRY

Weaving spiders, come not here;
   Hence, you long-legged spinners, hence!
Beetles black, approach not near;
   Worm nor snail, do no offense.

CHORUS

Philomel, with melody
   Sing in our sweet lullaby;
Lulla, lulla, lullaby, lulla, lulla, lullaby.
    Never harm
    Nor spell nor charm
  Come our lovely lady nigh.
  So good night, with lullaby.

                          [Titania sleeps.]

SECOND FAIRY

Hence, away! Now all is well.
One aloof stand sentinel.

                          [Exeunt Fairies.]

*Enter Oberon [and squeezes the flower on
Titania's eyelids].*

OBERON

What thou seest when thou dost wake,
Do it for thy true love take;
Love and languish for his sake.

---

11 Newts water lizards (considered poisonous, as were *blindworms*—
small snakes with tiny eyes—and spiders) **13 Philomel** the nightingale.
(Philomela, daughter of King Pandion, was transformed into a nightingale, according to Ovid's *Metamorphoses* 6, after she had been raped by
her sister Procne's husband, Tereus.)

Be it ounce, or cat, or bear, 36
Pard, or boar with bristled hair, 37
In thy eye that shall appear
When thou wak'st, it is thy dear.
Wake when some vile thing is near. [*Exit.*]

Enter Lysander and Hermia.

LYSANDER
Fair love, you faint with wandering in the wood;
   And to speak truth, I have forgot our way.
We'll rest us, Hermia, if you think it good,
   And tarry for the comfort of the day.

HERMIA
Be it so, Lysander. Find you out a bed,
For I upon this bank will rest my head.

LYSANDER
One turf shall serve as pillow for us both;
One heart, one bed, two bosoms, and one troth. 48

HERMIA
Nay, good Lysander, for my sake, my dear,
Lie further off yet; do not lie so near.

LYSANDER
O, take the sense, sweet, of my innocence! 51
Love takes the meaning in love's conference. 52
I mean that my heart unto yours is knit
So that but one heart we can make of it;
Two bosoms interchainèd with an oath—
So then two bosoms and a single troth.
Then by your side no bed-room me deny,
For lying so, Hermia, I do not lie. 58

HERMIA
Lysander riddles very prettily.
Now much beshrew my manners and my pride 60
If Hermia meant to say Lysander lied.
But, gentle friend, for love and courtesy
Lie further off, in human modesty; 63

36 ounce lynx   **37 Pard** leopard   **48 troth** faith, trothplight   **51 take . . . innocence** i.e., interpret my intention as innocent   **52 Love . . . conference** i.e., when lovers confer, love teaches each lover to interpret the other's meaning lovingly   **58 lie** tell a falsehood (with a riddling pun on *lie*, recline)   **60 beshrew** curse. (But mildly meant.)   **63 human** courteous

Such separation as may well be said
Becomes a virtuous bachelor and a maid,
So far be distant; and good night, sweet friend.
Thy love ne'er alter till thy sweet life end!

LYSANDER
Amen, amen, to that fair prayer, say I,
And then end life when I end loyalty!
Here is my bed. Sleep give thee all his rest!

HERMIA
With half that wish the wisher's eyes be pressed!   71
        [*They sleep, separated by a short distance.*]

        Enter Puck.

PUCK
Through the forest have I gone,
But Athenian found I none
On whose eyes I might approve   74
This flower's force in stirring love.
Night and silence.—Who is here?
Weeds of Athens he doth wear.
This is he, my master said,
Despisèd the Athenian maid;
And here the maiden, sleeping sound,
On the dank and dirty ground.
Pretty soul, she durst not lie
Near this lack-love, this kill-courtesy.
Churl, upon thy eyes I throw
All the power this charm doth owe.   85
        [*He applies the love juice.*]
When thou wak'st, let love forbid
Sleep his seat on thy eyelid.
So awake when I am gone,
For I must now to Oberon.   *Exit.*

        Enter Demetrius and Helena, running.

HELENA
Stay, though thou kill me, sweet Demetrius!
DEMETRIUS
I charge thee, hence, and do not haunt me thus.

---

71 With . . . pressed i.e., may we share your wish, so that your eyes too
are *pressed*, closed, in sleep   **74 approve** test   **85 owe** own

HELENA

O, wilt thou darkling leave me? Do not so.   92

DEMETRIUS

Stay, on thy peril! I alone will go.   [*Exit.*]   93

HELENA

O, I am out of breath in this fond chase!   94
The more my prayer, the lesser is my grace.   95
Happy is Hermia, wheresoe'er she lies,   96
For she hath blessèd and attractive eyes.
How came her eyes so bright? Not with salt tears;
If so, my eyes are oftener washed than hers.
No, no, I am as ugly as a bear;
For beasts that meet me run away for fear.
Therefore no marvel though Demetrius   102
Do, as a monster, fly my presence thus.   103
What wicked and dissembling glass of mine
Made me compare with Hermia's sphery eyne?   105
But who is here? Lysander, on the ground?
Dead, or asleep? I see no blood, no wound.
Lysander, if you live, good sir, awake.

LYSANDER [*Awaking*]

And run through fire I will for thy sweet sake.
Transparent Helena! Nature shows art,   110
That through thy bosom makes me see thy heart.
Where is Demetrius? O, how fit a word
Is that vile name to perish on my sword!

HELENA

Do not say so, Lysander, say not so.
What though he love your Hermia? Lord, what though?
Yet Hermia still loves you. Then be content.

LYSANDER

Content with Hermia? No! I do repent
The tedious minutes I with her have spent.
Not Hermia but Helena I love.
Who will not change a raven for a dove?
The will of man is by his reason swayed,

---

92 darkling in the dark   **93 on thy peril** i.e., on pain of danger to you if
you don't obey me and stay   **94 fond** doting   **95 my grace** the favor I
obtain   **96 lies** dwells   **102–103 no marvel . . . thus** i.e., no wonder that
Demetrius flies from me as from a monster   **105 compare** vie.   **sphery
eyne** eyes as bright as stars in their spheres   **110 Transparent** (1) radiant (2) able to be seen through

And reason says you are the worthier maid.
Things growing are not ripe until their season;
So I, being young, till now ripe not to reason.   124
And touching now the point of human skill,   125
Reason becomes the marshal to my will
And leads me to your eyes, where I o'erlook   127
Love's stories written in love's richest book.

HELENA
Wherefore was I to this keen mockery born?   129
When at your hands did I deserve this scorn?
Is 't not enough, is 't not enough, young man,
That I did never, no, nor never can,
Deserve a sweet look from Demetrius' eye,
But you must flout my insufficiency?
Good troth, you do me wrong, good sooth, you do,   135
In such disdainful manner me to woo.
But fare you well. Perforce I must confess
I thought you lord of more true gentleness.   138
O, that a lady, of one man refused,   139
Should of another therefore be abused!   *Exit.*   140

LYSANDER
She sees not Hermia. Hermia, sleep thou there,
And never mayst thou come Lysander near!
For as a surfeit of the sweetest things
The deepest loathing to the stomach brings,
Or as the heresies that men do leave   145
Are hated most of those they did deceive,   146
So thou, my surfeit and my heresy,
Of all be hated, but the most of me!
And, all my powers, address your love and might   149
To honor Helen and to be her knight!   *Exit.*

HERMIA [*Awaking*]
Help me, Lysander, help me! Do thy best
To pluck this crawling serpent from my breast!
Ay me, for pity! What a dream was here!
Lysander, look how I do quake with fear.

---

124 ripe not (am) not ripened   **125 touching** reaching.   **point** summit.
skill judgment   **127 o'erlook** read   **129 Wherefore** why   **135 Good
troth, good sooth** i.e., indeed, truly   **138 lord of** i.e., possessor of.
gentleness courtesy   **139 of** by   **140 abused** ill treated   **145–146 as . . .
deceive** as renounced heresies are hated most by those persons who
formerly were deceived by them   **149 address** direct, apply

Methought a serpent ate my heart away,
And you sat smiling at his cruel prey.   156
Lysander! What, removed? Lysander! Lord!
What, out of hearing? Gone? No sound, no word?
Alack, where are you? Speak, an if you hear;   159
Speak, of all loves! I swoon almost with fear.   160
No? Then I well perceive you are not nigh.
Either death, or you, I'll find immediately.
                    Exit. [*The sleeping Titania remains.*]

156 prey act of preying   **159 an if** if   **160 of loves** for all love's sake

3.1   *Enter the clowns [Quince, Snug, Bottom, Flute, Snout, and Starveling].*

BOTTOM   Are we all met?

QUINCE   Pat, pat; and here's a marvelous convenient   2
place for our rehearsal. This green plot shall be our
stage, this hawthorn brake our tiring-house, and we   4
will do it in action as we will do it before the Duke.

BOTTOM   Peter Quince?

QUINCE   What sayest thou, bully Bottom?   7

BOTTOM   There are things in this comedy of Pyramus
and Thisbe that will never please. First, Pyramus must
draw a sword to kill himself, which the ladies cannot
abide. How answer you that?

SNOUT   By 'r lakin, a parlous fear.   12

STARVELING   I believe we must leave the killing out,
when all is done.   14

BOTTOM   Not a whit. I have a device to make all well.
Write me a prologue, and let the prologue seem to say   16
we will do no harm with our swords, and that Pyramus
is not killed indeed; and for the more better assurance,
tell them that I, Pyramus, am not Pyramus but Bottom
the weaver. This will put them out of fear.

QUINCE   Well, we will have such a prologue, and it shall
be written in eight and six.   22

BOTTOM   No, make it two more; let it be written in eight
and eight.

SNOUT   Will not the ladies be afeard of the lion?

STARVELING   I fear it, I promise you.

BOTTOM   Masters, you ought to consider with yourselves, to bring in—God shield us!—a lion among la-   28
dies is a most dreadful thing. For there is not a more   29

3.1. Location: The action is continuous.
2 Pat on the dot, punctually   **4 brake** thicket.   **tiring-house** attiring
area, hence backstage   **7 bully** i.e., worthy, jolly, fine fellow   **12 By 'r
lakin** by our ladykin, i.e., the Virgin Mary.   **parlous** alarming   **14 when
all is done** i.e., when all is said and done   **16 Write me** i.e., write at my
suggestion. (*Me* is used colloquially.)   **22 eight and six** alternate lines of
eight and six syllables, a common ballad measure   **28–29 lion among
ladies** (A contemporary pamphlet tells how at the christening in 1594 of
Prince Henry, eldest son of King James VI of Scotland, later James I of
England, a "blackamoor" instead of a lion drew the triumphal chariot,
since the lion's presence might have "brought some fear to the nearest.")

fearful wildfowl than your lion living; and we ought 30
to look to 't.

SNOUT   Therefore another prologue must tell he is not a
lion.

BOTTOM   Nay, you must name his name, and half his
face must be seen through the lion's neck, and he himself must speak through, saying thus, or to the same
defect: "Ladies"—or "Fair ladies—I would wish 37
you"—or "I would request you"—or "I would entreat
you—not to fear, not to tremble; my life for yours. If 39
you think I come hither as a lion, it were pity of my 40
life. No, I am no such thing: I am a man as other men 41
are." And there indeed let him name his name and
tell them plainly he is Snug the joiner.

QUINCE   Well, it shall be so. But there is two hard things:
that is, to bring the moonlight into a chamber; for, you
know, Pyramus and Thisbe meet by moonlight.

SNOUT   Doth the moon shine that night we play our
play?

BOTTOM   A calendar, a calendar! Look in the almanac.
Find out moonshine, find out moonshine.

                          [*They consult an almanac.*]

QUINCE   Yes, it doth shine that night.

BOTTOM   Why, then, may you leave a casement of the
great chamber window, where we play, open, and the
moon may shine in at the casement.

QUINCE   Ay; or else one must come in with a bush of 55
thorns and a lantern and say he comes to disfigure, or 56
to present, the person of Moonshine. Then there is 57
another thing: we must have a wall in the great chamber; for Pyramus and Thisbe, says the story, did talk
through the chink of a wall.

SNOUT   You can never bring in a wall. What say you,
Bottom?

BOTTOM   Some man or other must present Wall. And let

---

30 fearful fear-inspiring   **37 defect** (Bottom's blunder for *effect*.)
39 my life for yours i.e., I pledge my life to make your lives safe
40–41 it were . . . life my life would be endangered   **55–56 bush of
thorns** bundle of thornbush faggots (part of the accoutrements of the
man in the moon, according to the popular notions of the time, along
with his lantern and his dog)   **56 disfigure** (Quince's blunder for *figure*.)   **57 present** represent

him have some plaster, or some loam, or some rough- 64
cast about him, to signify wall; or let him hold his 65
fingers thus, and through that cranny shall Pyramus
and Thisbe whisper.

QUINCE   If that may be, then all is well. Come, sit down,
every mother's son, and rehearse your parts. Pyramus,
you begin. When you have spoken your speech, enter
into that brake, and so everyone according to his cue.

Enter Robin [Puck].

PUCK
What hempen homespuns have we swaggering here   72
So near the cradle of the Fairy Queen?   73
What, a play toward? I'll be an auditor;   74
An actor too perhaps, if I see cause.
QUINCE   Speak, Pyramus. Thisbe, stand forth.
BOTTOM [*As Pyramus*]
"Thisbe, the flowers of odious savors sweet—"
QUINCE   Odors, odors.
BOTTOM   "—Odors savors sweet;
   So hath thy breath, my dearest Thisbe dear.
   But hark, a voice! Stay thou but here awhile,
   And by and by I will to thee appear."   *Exit.*
PUCK
A stranger Pyramus than e'er played here.   [*Exit.*] 83
FLUTE   Must I speak now?
QUINCE   Ay, marry, must you; for you must understand
he goes but to see a noise that he heard, and is to come
again.
FLUTE [*As Thisbe*]
"Most radiant Pyramus, most lily-white of hue,
   Of color like the red rose on triumphant brier,   89
Most brisky juvenal and eke most lovely Jew,   90

64–65 roughcast a mixture of lime and gravel used to plaster the outside of buildings   **72 hempen homespuns** i.e., rustics dressed in clothes
woven of coarse, homespun fabric made from hemp   **73 cradle** i.e.,
Titania's bower   **74 toward** about to take place   **83 A stranger . . . here**
(Puck indicates that he has conceived of his plan to present a "stranger"
Pyramus than ever seen before, and so Puck exits to put his plan into
effect.)   **89 triumphant** magnificent   **90 brisky juvenal** lively youth.
eke also.   **Jew** (Probably an absurd repetition of the first syllable of
juvenal, or Flute's error for *jewel*.)

As true as truest horse, that yet would never tire.
I'll meet thee, Pyramus, at Ninny's tomb."

QUINCE "Ninus' tomb," man. Why, you must not 93
speak that yet. That you answer to Pyramus. You
speak all your part at once, cues and all. Pyramus, en- 95
ter. Your cue is past; it is "never tire."

FLUTE
O—"As true as truest horse, that yet would never
tire."   97

[*Enter Puck, and Bottom as Pyramus with the ass
head.*]

BOTTOM
"If I were fair, Thisbe, I were only thine."   98

QUINCE O, monstrous! O, strange! We are haunted.
Pray, masters! Fly, masters! Help!
                              [*Exeunt Quince, Snug, Flute,
                                    Snout, and Starveling.*]

PUCK
I'll follow you, I'll lead you about a round,   101
  Through bog, through bush, through brake, through
    brier.
Sometimes a horse I'll be, sometimes a hound,
  A hog, a headless bear, sometimes a fire;   104
And neigh, and bark, and grunt, and roar, and burn,
Like horse, hound, hog, bear, fire, at every turn. *Exit.*

BOTTOM Why do they run away? This is a knavery of
them to make me afeard.

    Enter Snout.

SNOUT O Bottom, thou art changed! What do I see on
thee?

BOTTOM What do you see? You see an ass head of your
own, do you?   [*Exit Snout.*]

93 Ninus mythical founder of Nineveh (whose wife, Semiramis, was
supposed to have built the walls of Babylon where the story of Pyramus
and Thisbe takes place) **95 part** (An actor's *part* was a script consisting
only of his speeches and their cues.) **97 s.d. with the ass head** (This
stage direction, taken from the Folio, presumably refers to a standard
stage property.) **98 fair** handsome. **were** would be **101 about a
round** roundabout **104 fire** will-o'-the-wisp

Enter Quince.

QUINCE Bless thee, Bottom, bless thee! Thou art trans- 113
lated.   *Exit.* 114

BOTTOM I see their knavery. This is to make an ass of
me, to fright me, if they could. But I will not stir from
this place, do what they can. I will walk up and down
here, and will sing, that they shall hear I am not
afraid.   [*Sings.*]

   The ouzel cock so black of hue,   120
     With orange-tawny bill,
   The throstle with his note so true,   122
     The wren with little quill—   123

TITANIA [*Awaking*]
What angel wakes me from my flowery bed?

BOTTOM [*Sings*]
   The finch, the sparrow, and the lark,
     The plainsong cuckoo gray,   126
   Whose note full many a man doth mark,
     And dares not answer nay—   128
For, indeed, who would set his wit to so foolish a
bird? Who would give a bird the lie, though he cry 130
"cuckoo" never so?   131

TITANIA
I pray thee, gentle mortal, sing again.
Mine ear is much enamored of thy note;
So is mine eye enthrallèd to thy shape;
And thy fair virtue's force perforce doth move me   135
On the first view to say, to swear, I love thee.

BOTTOM Methinks, mistress, you should have little reason for that. And yet, to say the truth, reason and love
keep little company together nowadays. The more the
pity that some honest neighbors will not make them
friends. Nay, I can gleek upon occasion.   141

TITANIA
Thou art as wise as thou art beautiful.

113–114 translated transformed   **120 ouzel cock** male blackbird
122 throstle song thrush   **123 quill** (Literally, a reed pipe; hence, the
bird's piping song.)   **126 plainsong** singing a melody without variations   **128 dares . . . nay** i.e., cannot deny that he is a cuckold   **130 give
. . . lie** call the bird a liar   **131 never so** ever so much   **135 thy . . . force**
the power of your beauty   **141 gleek** scoff, jest

BOTTOM   Not so, neither. But if I had wit enough to get
  out of this wood, I have enough to serve mine own   144
  turn.   145

TITANIA
  Out of this wood do not desire to go.
  Thou shalt remain here, whether thou wilt or no.
  I am a spirit of no common rate.   148
  The summer still doth tend upon my state,   149
  And I do love thee. Therefore go with me.
  I'll give thee fairies to attend on thee,
  And they shall fetch thee jewels from the deep,
  And sing while thou on pressèd flowers dost sleep.
  And I will purge thy mortal grossness so   154
  That thou shalt like an airy spirit go.
  Peaseblossom, Cobweb, Mote, and Mustardseed!   156

    *Enter four Fairies [Peaseblossom, Cobweb, Mote,
    and Mustardseed].*

PEASEBLOSSOM   Ready.
COBWEB
  And I.
MOTE   And I.
MUSTARDSEED And I.
ALL   Where shall we go?
TITANIA
  Be kind and courteous to this gentleman.
  Hop in his walks and gambol in his eyes;   160
  Feed him with apricots and dewberries,   161
  With purple grapes, green figs, and mulberries;
  The honey bags steal from the humble-bees,
  And for night tapers crop their waxen thighs
  And light them at the fiery glowworms' eyes,
  To have my love to bed and to arise;
  And pluck the wings from painted butterflies
  To fan the moonbeams from his sleeping eyes.
  Nod to him, elves, and do him courtesies.

144–145 serve . . . turn answer my purpose   **148 rate** rank, value
149 still ever, always.   **doth . . . state** waits upon me as a part of my
royal retinue   **154 mortal grossness** materiality (i.e., the corporal nature
of a mortal being)   **156 Mote** i.e., speck. (The two words *moth* and *mote*
were pronounced alike, and both meanings may be present.)   **160 in his
eyes** in his sight (i.e., before him)   **161 dewberries** blackberries

PEASEBLOSSOM   Hail, mortal!

COBWEB   Hail!

MOTE   Hail!

MUSTARDSEED   Hail!

BOTTOM   I cry your worships mercy, heartily. I beseech
your worship's name.

COBWEB   Cobweb.

BOTTOM   I shall desire you of more acquaintance, good
Master Cobweb. If I cut my finger, I shall make bold   178
with you.—Your name, honest gentleman?   179

PEASEBLOSSOM   Peaseblossom.

BOTTOM   I pray you, commend me to Mistress Squash,   181
your mother, and to Master Peascod, your father.   182
Good Master Peaseblossom, I shall desire you of more
acquaintance too.—Your name, I beseech you, sir?

MUSTARDSEED   Mustardseed.

BOTTOM   Good Master Mustardseed, I know your pa-   186
tience well. That same cowardly, giantlike ox-beef   187
hath devoured many a gentleman of your house. I
promise you, your kindred hath made my eyes water   189
ere now. I desire you of more acquaintance, good
Master Mustardseed.

TITANIA

Come, wait upon him; lead him to my bower.
    The moon methinks looks with a watery eye;
And when she weeps, weeps every little flower,   194
    Lamenting some enforcèd chastity.   195
    Tie up my lover's tongue, bring him silently.   196

Exeunt.

❖

3.2   *Enter [Oberon,] King of Fairies.*

OBERON

I wonder if Titania be awaked;

178–179 **If . . . you** (Cobwebs were used to stanch bleeding.)   **181 Squash**
unripe pea pod   **182 Peascod** ripe pea pod   **186–187 your patience** what
you have endured   **189 water** (1) weep for sympathy (2) smart, sting
194 she weeps i.e., she causes dew   **195 enforcèd** forced, violated; or, possibly, constrained (since Titania at this moment is hardly concerned about
chastity)   **196 Tie . . . tongue** (Presumably Bottom is braying like an ass.)

3.2. Location: The wood.

Then what it was that next came in her eye,
Which she must dote on in extremity.

[*Enter*] *Robin Goodfellow* [*Puck*].

Here comes my messenger. How now, mad spirit?
What <u>night-rule</u> now about this <u>haunted</u> grove?   5

PUCK
My mistress with a monster is in love.
Near to her <u>close</u> and consecrated bower,   7
While she was in her <u>dull</u> and sleeping hour,   8
A crew of <u>patches</u>, <u>rude mechanicals</u>,   9
That work for bread upon Athenian <u>stalls</u>,   10
Were met together to rehearse a play
Intended for great Theseus' nuptial day.
The shallowest thick-skin of that <u>barren sort</u>,   13
Who Pyramus <u>presented</u> in their sport,   14
Forsook his <u>scene</u> and entered in a brake.   15
When I did him at this advantage take,
An ass's <u>noll</u> I fixèd on his head.   17
Anon his Thisbe must be answerèd,
And forth my <u>mimic</u> comes. When they him spy,   19
As wild geese that the creeping <u>fowler</u> eye,   20
Or <u>russet-pated choughs</u>, many <u>in sort</u>,   21
Rising and cawing at the gun's report,
<u>Sever</u> themselves and madly sweep the sky,   23
So, at his sight, away his fellows fly;
And, at our stamp, here o'er and o'er one falls;
He "Murder!" cries and help from Athens calls.
Their sense thus weak, lost with their fears thus strong,
Made senseless things begin to do them wrong,
For briers and thorns at their apparel snatch;
Some, sleeves—some, hats; <u>from yielders all things
catch</u>.   30

5 night-rule diversion for the night. **haunted** much frequented **7 close**
secret, private **8 dull** drowsy **9 patches** clowns, fools. **rude mechanicals** ignorant artisans **10 stalls** market booths **13 barren sort** stupid
company or crew **14 presented** acted **15 scene** playing area **17 noll**
noddle, head **19 mimic** burlesque actor **20 fowler** hunter of game
birds **21 russet-pated choughs** reddish brown or gray-headed jack-
daws. **in sort** in a flock **23 Sever** i.e., scatter **30 from . . . catch** i.e.,
everything preys on those who yield to fear

I led them on in this distracted fear
And left sweet Pyramus translated there,
When in that moment, so it came to pass,
Titania waked and straightway loved an ass.

OBERON
This falls out better than I could devise.
But hast thou yet <u>latched</u> the Athenian's eyes   36
With the love juice, as I did bid thee do?

PUCK
I took him sleeping—that is finished too—
And the Athenian woman by his side,
That, when he waked, <u>of force</u> she must be eyed.   40

Enter Demetrius and Hermia.

OBERON
Stand close. This is the same Athenian.

PUCK
This is the woman, but not this the man.
                              [*They stand aside.*]

DEMETRIUS
O, why rebuke you him that loves you so?
Lay breath so bitter on your bitter foe.

HERMIA
Now I but chide; but I should use thee worse,
For thou, I fear, hast given me cause to curse.
If thou hast slain Lysander in his sleep,
Being <u>o'er shoes</u> in blood, plunge in the deep,   48
And kill me too.
The sun was not so true unto the day
As he to me. Would he have stolen away
From sleeping Hermia? I'll believe as soon
This <u>whole</u> earth may be bored, and that the moon   53
May through the center creep, and so displease
<u>Her brother</u>'s noontide with <u>th' Antipodes.</u>   55
It cannot be but thou hast murdered him;
So should a murderer look, so <u>dead,</u> so grim.   57

---

36 latched fastened, snared **40 of force** perforce **48 o'er shoes** i.e., so far gone **53 whole** solid **55 Her brother's** i.e., the sun's. **th' Antipodes** the people on the opposite side of the earth (where the moon is imagined bringing night to noontime) **57 dead** deadly, or deathly pale

DEMETRIUS

  So should the murdered look, and so should I,
  Pierced through the heart with your stern cruelty.
  Yet you, the murderer, look as bright, as clear,
  As yonder Venus in her glimmering sphere.

HERMIA

  What's this _to my Lysander? Where is he?   62
  Ah, good Demetrius, wilt thou give him me?

DEMETRIUS

  I had rather give his carcass to my hounds.

HERMIA

  Out, dog! Out, cur! Thou driv'st me past the bounds
  Of maiden's patience. Hast thou slain him, then?
  Henceforth be never numbered among men.
  O, once tell true, tell true, even for my sake:
  Durst thou have looked upon him being awake?
  And hast thou killed him sleeping? O _brave touch!_   70
  Could not a _worm,_ an adder, do so much?   71
  An adder did it; for with doubler tongue
  Than thine, thou serpent, never adder stung.

DEMETRIUS

  You spend your _passion_ on a _misprised mood._   74
  I am not guilty of Lysander's blood,
  Nor is he dead, for aught that I can tell.

HERMIA

  I pray thee, tell me then that he is well.

DEMETRIUS

  An if I could, what should I get therefor?

HERMIA

  A privilege never to see me more.
  And from thy hated presence part I so.
  See me no more, whether he be dead or no.   _Exit._

DEMETRIUS

  There is no following her in this fierce vein.
  Here therefore for a while I will remain.
  So sorrow's heaviness doth _heavier_ grow   84
  For debt that _bankrupt_ sleep doth sorrow owe; 85

---

62 to to do with **70 brave touch** noble exploit. (Said ironically.) **71 worm**
serpent **74 passion** violent feelings. **misprised mood** anger based on mis-
conception **84 heavier** (1) harder to bear (2) more drowsy **85 bankrupt** (Demetrius is saying that his sleepiness adds to the weariness caused by sorrow.)

Which now in some slight measure it will pay,   86
If for his tender here I make some stay.   87

Lie[s] down [and sleeps].

OBERON
What hast thou done? Thou hast mistaken quite
And laid the love juice on some true love's sight.
Of thy misprision must perforce ensue   90
Some true love turned, and not a false turned true.

PUCK
Then fate o'errules, that, one man holding troth,   92
A million fail, confounding oath on oath.   93

OBERON
About the wood go swifter than the wind,
And Helena of Athens look thou find.   95
All fancy-sick she is and pale of cheer   96
With sighs of love, that cost the fresh blood dear.   97
By some illusion see thou bring her here.
I'll charm his eyes against she do appear.   99

PUCK
I go, I go, look how I go,
Swifter than arrow from the Tartar's bow.   101

[Exit.]

OBERON [*Applying love juice to Demetrius' eyes*]
Flower of this purple dye,
Hit with Cupid's archery,
Sink in apple of his eye.
When his love he doth espy,
Let her shine as gloriously
As the Venus of the sky.
When thou wak'st, if she be by,
Beg of her for remedy.

Enter Puck.

86–87 Which . . . stay i.e., to a small extent I will be able to
"pay back" and hence find some relief from sorrow, if I pause here
awhile (*make some stay*) while sleep "tenders" or offers itself by
way of paying the debt owed to sorrow   **90 misprision** mistake   **92 troth** faith   **93 confounding . . . oath** i.e., invalidating
one oath with another   **95 look** i.e., be sure   **96 fancy-sick** love-
sick.   **cheer** face   **97 sighs . . . blood** (An allusion to the physio-
logical theory that each sigh costs the heart a drop of blood.)
99 against . . . appear in anticipation of her coming   **101 Tartar's
bow** (Tartars were famed for their skill with the bow.)

PUCK

> Captain of our fairy band,
> Helena is here at hand,
> And the youth, mistook by me,
> Pleading for a lover's fee.   113
> Shall we their fond pageant see?   114
> Lord, what fools these mortals be!

OBERON

> Stand aside. The noise they make
> Will cause Demetrius to awake.

PUCK

> Then will two at once woo one;
> That must needs be sport alone.   119
> And those things do best please me
> That befall preposterously.   121

> > > > > *[They stand aside.]*

Enter Lysander and Helena.

LYSANDER

> Why should you think that I should woo in scorn?
>   Scorn and derision never come in tears.
> Look when I vow, I weep; and vows so born,   124
>   In their nativity all truth appears.   125
> How can these things in me seem scorn to you,
> Bearing the badge of faith to prove them true?   127

HELENA

> You do advance your cunning more and more.   128
>   When truth kills truth, O, devilish-holy fray!   129
> These vows are Hermia's. Will you give her o'er?
>   Weigh oath with oath, and you will nothing weigh.
> Your vows to her and me, put in two scales,
> Will even weigh, and both as light as tales.   133

LYSANDER

> I had no judgment when to her I swore.

---

113 fee privilege, reward   **114 fond pageant** foolish exhibition
119 alone unequaled   **121 preposterously** out of the natural order
124 Look when whenever   **124–125 vows . . . appears** i.e., vows made by
one who is weeping give evidence thereby of their sincerity   **127 badge**
identifying device such as that worn on servants' livery (here, his
tears)   **128 advance** carry forward, display   **129 truth kills truth** i.e.,
one of Lysander's vows must invalidate the other   **133 tales** lies

HELENA
  Nor none, in my mind, now you give her o'er.
LYSANDER
  Demetrius loves her, and he loves not you.
DEMETRIUS [*Awaking*]
  O Helen, goddess, nymph, perfect, divine!
  To what, my love, shall I compare thine eyne?
  Crystal is muddy. O, how ripe in show   139
  Thy lips, those kissing cherries, tempting grow!
  That pure congealèd white, high Taurus' snow,   141
  Fanned with the eastern wind, turns to a crow   142
  When thou hold'st up thy hand. O, let me kiss
  This princess of pure white, this seal of bliss!   144
HELENA
  O spite! O hell! I see you all are bent
  To set against me for your merriment.   146
  If you were civil and knew courtesy,
  You would not do me thus much injury.
  Can you not hate me, as I know you do,
  But you must join in souls to mock me too?
  If you were men, as men you are in show,
  You would not use a gentle lady so—
  To vow, and swear, and superpraise my parts,   153
  When I am sure you hate me with your hearts.
  You both are rivals, and love Hermia;
  And now both rivals, to mock Helena.
  A trim exploit, a manly enterprise,   157
  To conjure tears up in a poor maid's eyes
  With your derision! None of noble sort   159
  Would so offend a virgin and extort   160
  A poor soul's patience, all to make you sport.
LYSANDER
  You are unkind, Demetrius. Be not so;
  For you love Hermia; this you know I know.
  And here, with all good will, with all my heart,
  In Hermia's love I yield you up my part;

139 show appearance   **141 Taurus** a lofty mountain range in Asia
Minor   **142 turns to a crow** i.e., seems black by contrast   **144 seal**
pledge   **146 set against** attack   **153 superpraise** overpraise.   **parts**
qualities   **157 trim** pretty, fine. (Said ironically.)   **159 sort** character,
quality   **160 extort** twist, torture

And yours of Helena to me bequeath,
Whom I do love and will do till my death.

HELENA
Never did mockers waste more idle breath.

DEMETRIUS
Lysander, keep thy Hermia; I will none.   169
If e'er I loved her, all that love is gone.
My heart to her but as guest-wise sojourned,   171
And now to Helen is it home returned,
There to remain.

LYSANDER   Helen, it is not so.

DEMETRIUS
Disparage not the faith thou dost not know,
Lest, to thy peril, thou aby it dear.   175
Look where thy love comes; yonder is thy dear.

Enter Hermia.

HERMIA
Dark night, that from the eye his function takes,   177
The ear more quick of apprehension makes;
Wherein it doth impair the seeing sense,
It pays the hearing double recompense.
Thou art not by mine eye, Lysander, found;
Mine ear, I thank it, brought me to thy sound.
But why unkindly didst thou leave me so?

LYSANDER
Why should he stay whom love doth press to go?

HERMIA
What love could press Lysander from my side?

LYSANDER
Lysander's love, that would not let him bide—
Fair Helena, who more engilds the night   187
Than all yon fiery oes and eyes of light.   188
Why seek'st thou me? Could not this make thee know,
The hate I bear thee made me leave thee so?

HERMIA
You speak not as you think. It cannot be.

HELENA
Lo, she is one of this confederacy!

169 will none i.e., want no part of her   **171 to . . . sojourned** only visited
with her   **175 aby** pay for   **177 his** its   **187 engilds** brightens with a
golden light   **188 oes** spangles (here, stars)

Now I perceive they have conjoined all three
To fashion this false sport in spite of me.   194
Injurious Hermia, most ungrateful maid!
Have you conspired, have you with these contrived   196
To bait me with this foul derision?   197
Is all the counsel that we two have shared,   198
The sisters' vows, the hours that we have spent,
When we have chid the hasty-footed time
For parting us—O, is all forgot?
All schooldays' friendship, childhood innocence?
We, Hermia, like two artificial gods,   203
Have with our needles created both one flower,
Both on one sampler, sitting on one cushion,
Both warbling of one song, both in one key,
As if our hands, our sides, voices, and minds
Had been incorporate. So we grew together   208
Like to a double cherry, seeming parted
But yet an union in partition,
Two lovely berries molded on one stem;   211
So with two seeming bodies but one heart,
Two of the first, like coats in heraldry,   213
Due but to one and crownèd with one crest.   214
And will you rend our ancient love asunder
To join with men in scorning your poor friend?
It is not friendly, 'tis not maidenly.
Our sex, as well as I, may chide you for it,
Though I alone do feel the injury.

HERMIA
I am amazèd at your passionate words.
I scorn you not. It seems that you scorn me.

HELENA
Have you not set Lysander, as in scorn,
To follow me and praise my eyes and face?
And made your other love, Demetrius,
Who even but now did spurn me with his foot,
To call me goddess, nymph, divine and rare,

194 **in spite of me** to vex me   196 **contrived** plotted   197 **bait** torment,
as one sets on dogs to bait a bear   198 **counsel** confidential talk
203 **artificial** skilled in art or creation   208 **incorporate** of one body
211 **lovely** loving   213–214 **Two . . . crest** i.e., we have two separate
bodies, just as a coat of arms in heraldry can be represented twice on a
shield but surmounted by a single crest

Precious, celestial? Wherefore speaks he this
To her he hates? And wherefore doth Lysander
Deny your love, so rich within his soul,
And tender me, forsooth, affection,   230
But by your setting on, by your consent?
What though I be not so in grace as you,   232
So hung upon with love, so fortunate,
But miserable most, to love unloved?
This you should pity rather than despise.

HERMIA
I understand not what you mean by this.

HELENA
Ay, do! Persever, counterfeit sad looks,   237
Make mouths upon me when I turn my back,   238
Wink each at other, hold the sweet jest up.   239
This sport, well carried, shall be chronicled.   240
If you have any pity, grace, or manners,
You would not make me such an argument.   242
But fare ye well. 'Tis partly my own fault,
Which death, or absence, soon shall remedy.

LYSANDER
Stay, gentle Helena; hear my excuse,
My love, my life, my soul, fair Helena!

HELENA
O excellent!

HERMIA [*To Lysander*]   Sweet, do not scorn her so.

DEMETRIUS
If she cannot entreat, I can compel.   248

LYSANDER
Thou canst compel no more than she entreat.
Thy threats have no more strength than her weak
    prayers.
Helen, I love thee, by my life, I do!
I swear by that which I will lose for thee,
To prove him false that says I love thee not.

DEMETRIUS
I say I love thee more than he can do.

---

230 tender offer   **232 grace** favor   **237 sad** grave, serious   **238 mouths**
i.e., mows, faces, grimaces.   **upon** at   **239 hold . . . up** keep up the
joke   **240 carried** managed   **242 argument** subject for a jest   **248 entreat** i.e., succeed by entreaty

LYSANDER
  If thou say so, withdraw, and prove it too.
DEMETRIUS
  Quick, come!
HERMIA   Lysander, whereto tends all this?
LYSANDER
  Away, you Ethiop!
      [*He tries to break away from Hermia.*]
DEMETRIUS   No, no; he'll   257
  Seem to break loose; take on as you would follow,   258
  But yet come not. You are a tame man, go!
LYSANDER
  Hang off, thou cat, thou burr! Vile thing, let loose,   260
  Or I will shake thee from me like a serpent!
HERMIA
  Why are you grown so rude? What change is this,
  Sweet love?
LYSANDER   Thy love? Out, tawny Tartar, out!
  Out, loathèd med'cine! O hated potion, hence!   264
HERMIA
  Do you not jest?
HELENA   Yes, sooth, and so do you.   265
LYSANDER
  Demetrius, I will keep my word with thee.
DEMETRIUS
  I would I had your bond, for I perceive
  A weak bond holds you. I'll not trust your word.   268
LYSANDER
  What, should I hurt her, strike her, kill her dead?
  Although I hate her, I'll not harm her so.
HERMIA
  What, can you do me greater harm than hate?
  Hate me? Wherefore? O me, what news, my love?   272
  Am not I Hermia? Are not you Lysander?
  I am as fair now as I was erewhile.   274
  Since night you loved me; yet since night you left me.

257 Ethiop (Referring to Hermia's relatively dark hair and complexion; see also *tawny Tartar* six lines later.)   **258 take on as** act as if   **260 Hang off** let go   **264 med'cine** i.e., poison   **265 sooth** truly   **268 weak bond** i.e., Hermia's arm (with a pun on *bond*, oath, in the previous line)   **272 what news** what is the matter   **274 erewhile** just now

Why, then you left me—O, the gods forbid!—
In earnest, shall I say?

LYSANDER   Ay, by my life!
And never did desire to see thee more.
Therefore be out of hope, of question, of doubt;
Be certain, nothing truer. 'Tis no jest
That I do hate thee and love Helena.

HERMIA [*To Helena*]
O me! You juggler! You cankerblossom!   282
You thief of love! What, have you come by night
And stol'n my love's heart from him?

HELENA   Fine, i' faith!
Have you no modesty, no maiden shame,
No touch of bashfulness? What, will you tear
Impatient answers from my gentle tongue?
Fie, fie! You counterfeit, you puppet, you!   288

HERMIA
"Puppet"? Why, so! Ay, that way goes the game.   289
Now I perceive that she hath made compare
Between our statures; she hath urged her height,
And with her personage, her tall personage,
Her height, forsooth, she hath prevailed with him.
And are you grown so high in his esteem
Because I am so dwarfish and so low?
How low am I, thou painted maypole? Speak!
How low am I? I am not yet so low
But that my nails can reach unto thine eyes.
                    [*She flails at Helena but is restrained.*]

HELENA
I pray you, though you mock me, gentlemen,
Let her not hurt me. I was never curst;   300
I have no gift at all in shrewishness;
I am a right maid for my cowardice.   302
Let her not strike me. You perhaps may think,
Because she is something lower than myself,   304
That I can match her.

HERMIA   Lower? Hark, again!

---

282 cankerblossom worm that destroys the flower bud (?) **288 puppet**
(1) counterfeit (2) dwarfish woman (in reference to Hermia's smaller
stature) **289 Why, so** i.e., Oh, so that's how it is **300 curst** shrewish
302 right true **304 something** somewhat

HELENA
Good Hermia, do not be so bitter with me.
I evermore did love you, Hermia,
Did ever keep your counsels, never wronged you;
Save that, in love unto Demetrius,
I told him of your stealth unto this wood.   310
He followed you; for love I followed him.
But he hath chid me hence and threatened me   312
To strike me, spurn me, nay, to kill me too.
And now, so you will let me quiet go,   314
To Athens will I bear my folly back
And follow you no further. Let me go.
You see how simple and how fond I am.   317

HERMIA
Why, get you gone. Who is 't that hinders you?

HELENA
A foolish heart, that I leave here behind.

HERMIA
What, with Lysander?

HELENA   With Demetrius.

LYSANDER
Be not afraid; she shall not harm thee, Helena.

DEMETRIUS
No, sir, she shall not, though you take her part.

HELENA
O, when she is angry, she is keen and shrewd.   323
She was a vixen when she went to school,
And though she be but little, she is fierce.

HERMIA
"Little" again? Nothing but "low" and "little"?
Why will you suffer her to flout me thus?
Let me come to her.

LYSANDER   Get you gone, you dwarf!
You minimus, of hindering knotgrass made!   329
You bead, you acorn!

DEMETRIUS   You are too officious
In her behalf that scorns your services.
Let her alone. Speak not of Helena;

---

310 stealth stealing away   **312 chid me hence** driven me away with his
scolding   **314 so** if only   **317 fond** foolish   **323 keen** fierce, cruel.
shrewd shrewish   **329 minimus** diminutive creature.   **knotgrass** a
weed, an infusion of which was thought to stunt the growth

Take not her part. For, if thou dost intend   333
Never so little show of love to her,
Thou shalt aby it.

LYSANDER   Now she holds me not;   335
Now follow, if thou dar'st, to try whose right,
Of thine or mine, is most in Helena.   [*Exit.*]

DEMETRIUS
Follow? Nay, I'll go with thee, cheek by jowl.   338
          [*Exit, following Lysander.*]

HERMIA
You, mistress, all this coil is 'long of you.   339
Nay, go not back.

HELENA   I will not trust you, I,   340
Nor longer stay in your curst company.
Your hands than mine are quicker for a fray;
My legs are longer, though, to run away.   [*Exit.*]

HERMIA
I am amazed and know not what to say.   *Exit.*

[*Oberon and Puck come forward.*]

OBERON
This is thy negligence. Still thou mistak'st,
Or else committ'st thy knaveries willfully.

PUCK
Believe me, king of shadows, I mistook.
Did not you tell me I should know the man
By the Athenian garments he had on?
And so far blameless proves my enterprise
That I have 'nointed an Athenian's eyes;
And so far am I glad it so did sort,   352
As this their jangling I esteem a sport.   353

OBERON
Thou seest these lovers seek a place to fight.
Hie therefore, Robin, overcast the night;   355
The starry welkin cover thou anon   356
With drooping fog as black as Acheron,   357
And lead these testy rivals so astray

333 **intend** give sign of   335 **aby** pay for   338 **cheek by jowl** i.e., side by
side   339 **coil** turmoil, dissension.   **'long of** on account of   340 **go not
back** i.e., don't retreat. (Hermia is again proposing a fight.)   352 **sort**
turn out   353 **As** that (also at l. 359)   355 **Hie** hasten   356 **welkin** sky
357 **Acheron** river of Hades (here representing Hades itself)

As one come not within another's way.
Like to Lysander sometimes frame thy tongue,
Then stir Demetrius up with bitter wrong;   361
And sometimes rail thou like Demetrius.
And from each other look thou lead them thus,
Till o'er their brows death-counterfeiting sleep
With leaden legs and batty wings doth creep.   365
Then crush this herb into Lysander's eye,   366

[Giving herb]

Whose liquor hath this virtuous property,   367
To take from thence all error with his might   368
And make his eyeballs roll with wonted sight.   369
When they next wake, all this derision   370
Shall seem a dream and fruitless vision,
And back to Athens shall the lovers wend
With league whose date till death shall never end.   373
Whiles I in this affair do thee employ,
I'll to my queen and beg her Indian boy;
And then I will her charmèd eye release
From monster's view, and all things shall be peace.

PUCK
My fairy lord, this must be done with haste,
For night's swift dragons cut the clouds full fast,   379
And yonder shines Aurora's harbinger,   380
At whose approach, ghosts, wand'ring here and there,
Troop home to churchyards. Damnèd spirits all,
That in crossways and floods have burial,   383
Already to their wormy beds are gone.
For fear lest day should look their shames upon,
They willfully themselves exile from light
And must for aye consort with black-browed night.   387
OBERON
But we are spirits of another sort.

361 wrong insults **365 batty** batlike **366 this herb** i.e., the antidote
(mentioned in 2.1.184) to love-in-idleness **367 virtuous** efficacious
368 his its **369 wonted** accustomed **370 derision** laughable business
373 date term of existence **379 dragons** (Supposed by Shakespeare to
be yoked to the car of the goddess of night.) **380 Aurora's harbinger**
the morning star, precursor of dawn **383 crossways . . . burial** (Those
who had committed suicide were buried at crossways, with a stake
driven through them; those drowned, i.e., buried in floods or great
waters, would be condemned to wander disconsolate for want of burial
rites.) **387 for aye** forever

I with the Morning's love have oft made sport,   389
And, like a forester, the groves may tread   390
Even till the eastern gate, all fiery red,
Opening on Neptune with fair blessèd beams,
Turns into yellow gold his salt green streams.
But notwithstanding, haste, make no delay.
We may effect this business yet ere day.   [*Exit.*]

PUCK
      Up and down, up and down,
      I will lead them up and down.
      I am feared in field and town.
      Goblin, lead them up and down.
Here comes one.

    Enter Lysander.

LYSANDER
Where art thou, proud Demetrius? Speak thou now.
PUCK [*Mimicking Demetrius*]
Here, villain, drawn and ready. Where art thou?   402
LYSANDER
I will be with thee straight.
PUCK   Follow me, then,   403
To plainer ground.
    [*Lysander wanders about, following the voice.*]

    Enter Demetrius.

DEMETRIUS   Lysander! Speak again!   404
Thou runaway, thou coward, art thou fled?
Speak! In some bush? Where dost thou hide thy head?
PUCK [*Mimicking Lysander*]
Thou coward, art thou bragging to the stars,
Telling the bushes that thou look'st for wars,
And wilt not come? Come, recreant; come, thou child,   409
I'll whip thee with a rod. He is defiled
That draws a sword on thee.
DEMETRIUS   Yea, art thou there?

---

389 Morning's love Cephalus, a beautiful youth beloved by Aurora; or
perhaps the goddess of the dawn herself   **390 forester** keeper of a royal
forest   **402 drawn** with drawn sword   **403 straight** immediately
404 plainer more open   **s.d. Lysander wanders about** (It is not
clearly necessary that Lysander exit at this point; neither exit nor
reentrance is indicated in the early texts.)   **409 recreant** cowardly wretch

PUCK
Follow my voice. We'll <u>try</u> no manhood here.   412
                                        Exeunt.

    [*Lysander returns.*]

LYSANDER
He goes before me and still dares me on.
When I come where he calls, then he is gone.
The villain is much lighter-heeled than I.
I followed fast, but faster he did fly,
That fallen am I in dark uneven way,
And here will rest me. [*He lies down.*] Come, thou gentle
    day!
For if but once thou show me thy gray light,
I'll find Demetrius and revenge this spite. [*He sleeps.*]

    [*Enter*] Robin [*Puck*] *and Demetrius.*

PUCK
Ho, ho, ho! Coward, why com'st thou not?
DEMETRIUS
<u>Abide</u> me, if thou dar'st; for well I <u>wot</u>   422
Thou runn'st before me, shifting every place,
And dar'st not stand nor look me in the face.
Where art thou now?
PUCK   Come hither. I am here.
DEMETRIUS
Nay, then, thou mock'st me. Thou shalt <u>buy</u> this <u>dear,</u>   426
If ever I thy face by daylight see.
Now, go thy way. Faintness constraineth me
To measure out my length on this cold bed.
By day's approach look to be visited.
                        [*He lies down and sleeps.*]

    Enter Helena.

HELENA
O weary night, O long and tedious night,
    <u>Abate</u> thy hours! Shine comforts from the east,   432
That I may back to Athens by daylight,
    From these that my poor company detest;

412 try test **422 Abide** confront, face. **wot** know **426 buy** aby, pay
for. **dear** dearly **432 Abate** lessen, shorten

And sleep, that sometimes shuts up sorrow's eye,
Steal me awhile from mine own company.

[She lies down and] sleep[s].

PUCK

    Yet but three? Come one more;
    Two of both kinds makes up four.
    Here she comes, <u>curst</u> and sad.   439
    Cupid is a knavish lad,
    Thus to make poor females mad.

    [Enter Hermia.]

HERMIA

Never so weary, never so in woe,
  Bedabbled with the dew and torn with briers,
I can no further crawl, no further go;
  My legs can keep no pace with my desires.
Here will I rest me till the break of day.
Heavens shield Lysander, if they mean a fray!

    [She lies down and sleeps.]

PUCK

      On the ground
      Sleep sound.
      I'll apply
      To your eye,
    Gentle lover, remedy.

        [Squeezing the juice on Lysander's eyes.]
      When thou wak'st,
      Thou tak'st
      True delight
      In the sight
    Of thy former lady's eye;
    And the country proverb known,
    That every man should take his own,
    In your waking shall be shown:
    <u>Jack shall have Jill;</u>   461
      Naught shall go ill;
    The man shall have his mare again, and all shall be
    well.   *[Exit. The four sleeping lovers remain.]*

439 curst ill-tempered   **461 Jack shall have Jill** (Proverbial for "boy gets girl.")

4.1   *Enter [Titania,] Queen of Fairies, and [Bottom
the] clown, and Fairies; and [Oberon,] the King,
behind them.*

TITANIA
Come, sit thee down upon this flowery bed,
    While I thy amiable cheeks do coy,   2
And stick muskroses in thy sleek smooth head,
    And kiss thy fair large ears, my gentle joy.
                                    [They recline.]
BOTTOM   Where's Peaseblossom?
PEASEBLOSSOM   Ready.
BOTTOM   Scratch my head, Peaseblossom. Where's
Monsieur Cobweb?
COBWEB   Ready.
BOTTOM   Monsieur Cobweb, good monsieur, get you
your weapons in your hand, and kill me a red-hipped
humble-bee on the top of a thistle; and, good mon-
sieur, bring me the honey bag. Do not fret yourself
too much in the action, monsieur; and, good mon-
sieur, have a care the honey bag break not; I would be
loath to have you overflown with a honey bag, si-
gnor. [*Exit Cobweb.*] Where's Monsieur Mustardseed?
MUSTARDSEED   Ready.
BOTTOM   Give me your neaf, Monsieur Mustardseed.   19
Pray you, leave your courtesy, good monsieur.   20
MUSTARDSEED   What's your will?
BOTTOM   Nothing, good monsieur, but to help Caval-   22
ery Cobweb to scratch. I must to the barber's, mon-   23
sieur, for methinks I am marvelous hairy about the
face; and I am such a tender ass, if my hair do but
tickle me, I must scratch.
TITANIA
What, wilt thou hear some music, my sweet love?

**4.1. Location: The action is continuous. The four lovers are still asleep
onstage.**
2 amiable lovely.   **coy** caress   **19 neaf** fist   **20 leave your courtesy** i.e.,
stop bowing, or put on your hat   **22–23 Cavalery** cavalier. (Form of
address for a gentleman.)   **23 Cobweb** (Seemingly an error, since Cobweb has been sent to bring honey while Peaseblossom has been asked to
scratch.)

BOTTOM I have a reasonable good ear in music. Let's
have the tongs and the bones.   29

[Music: tongs, rural music.]

TITANIA
  Or say, sweet love, what thou desirest to eat.

BOTTOM Truly, a peck of provender. I could munch 31
your good dry oats. Methinks I have a great desire to
a bottle of hay. Good hay, sweet hay, hath no fellow. 33

TITANIA
  I have a venturous fairy that shall seek
  The squirrel's hoard, and fetch thee new nuts.

BOTTOM I had rather have a handful or two of dried
peas. But, I pray you, let none of your people stir me. 37
I have an exposition of sleep come upon me. 38

TITANIA
  Sleep thou, and I will wind thee in my arms.
  Fairies, begone, and be all ways away. 40

[Exeunt Fairies.]

  So doth the woodbine the sweet honeysuckle
  Gently entwist; the female ivy so
  Enrings the barky fingers of the elm.
  O, how I love thee! How I dote on thee!

[They sleep.]

Enter Robin Goodfellow [Puck].

OBERON *[Coming forward]*
  Welcome, good Robin. Seest thou this sweet sight?
  Her dotage now I do begin to pity.
  For, meeting her of late behind the wood,
  Seeking sweet favors for this hateful fool, 48
  I did upbraid her and fall out with her.
  For she his hairy temples then had rounded
  With coronet of fresh and fragrant flowers;
  And that same dew, which sometime on the buds 52

29 tongs . . . bones instruments for rustic music. (The tongs were played like a triangle, whereas the bones were held between the fingers and used as clappers.) **s.d. Music . . . music** (This stage direction is added from the Folio.) **31 peck of provender** one-quarter bushel of grain **33 bottle** bundle. **fellow** equal **37 stir** disturb **38 exposition** (Bottom's word for *disposition*.) **40 all ways** in all directions **48 favors** i.e., gifts of flowers **52 sometime** formerly

Was wont to swell like round and orient pearls,   53
Stood now within the pretty flowerets' eyes
Like tears that did their own disgrace bewail.
When I had at my pleasure taunted her,
And she in mild terms begged my patience,
I then did ask of her her changeling child,
Which straight she gave me, and her fairy sent
To bear him to my bower in Fairyland.
And, now I have the boy, I will undo
This hateful imperfection of her eyes.
And, gentle Puck, take this transformèd scalp
From off the head of this Athenian swain,
That he, awaking when the other do,   65
May all to Athens back again repair,   66
And think no more of this night's accidents
But as the fierce vexation of a dream.
But first I will release the Fairy Queen.
          [*He squeezes a herb on her eyes.*]
     Be as thou wast wont to be;
     See as thou wast wont to see.
     Dian's bud o'er Cupid's flower   72
     Hath such force and blessèd power.
Now, my Titania, wake you, my sweet queen.
TITANIA [*Waking*]
   My Oberon! What visions have I seen!
   Methought I was enamored of an ass.
OBERON
   There lies your love.
TITANIA   How came these things to pass?
   O, how mine eyes do loathe his visage now!
OBERON
   Silence awhile. Robin, take off this head.
   Titania, music call, and strike more dead
   Than common sleep of all these five the sense.   81

53 orient pearls i.e., the most beautiful of all pearls, those coming from the Orient   **65 other** others   **66 repair** return   **72 Dian's bud** (Perhaps the flower of the *agnus castus* or chaste-tree, supposed to preserve chastity; or perhaps referring simply to Oberon's herb by which he can undo the effects of "Cupid's flower," the love-in-idleness of 2.1.166–168.)   **81 these five** i.e., the four lovers and Bottom

TITANIA
    Music, ho! Music, such as charmeth sleep!   82
                                        [*Music.*]
PUCK [*Removing the ass head*]
    Now, when thou wak'st, with thine own fool's eyes peep.
OBERON
    Sound, music! Come, my queen, take hands with me,
    And rock the ground whereon these sleepers be.
                                        [*They dance.*]
    Now thou and I are new in amity,
    And will tomorrow midnight solemnly   87
    Dance in Duke Theseus' house triumphantly,
    And bless it to all fair prosperity.
    There shall the pairs of faithful lovers be
    Wedded, with Theseus, all in jollity.
PUCK
        Fairy King, attend, and mark:
        I do hear the morning lark.
OBERON
        Then, my queen, in silence sad,   94
        Trip we after night's shade.
        We the globe can compass soon,
        Swifter than the wandering moon.
TITANIA
        Come, my lord, and in our flight
        Tell me how it came this night
        That I sleeping here was found
        With these mortals on the ground.   *Exeunt.*
                                        Wind horn [*within*].

    Enter Theseus and all his train; [*Hippolyta,*
    Egeus].

THESEUS
    Go, one of you, find out the forester,
    For now our observation is performed;   103
    And since we have the vaward of the day,   104
    My love shall hear the music of my hounds.

---

82 charmeth brings about, as though by a charm   **87 solemnly** ceremo-
niously   **94 sad** sober   **103 observation** i.e., observance to a morn of
May (1.1.167)   **104 vaward** vanguard, i.e., earliest part

Uncouple in the western valley, let them go.   106
Dispatch, I say, and find the forester.

                [*Exit an Attendant.*]

We will, fair queen, up to the mountain's top
And mark the musical confusion
Of hounds and echo in conjunction.

HIPPOLYTA

I was with Hercules and Cadmus once,   111
When in a wood of Crete they bayed the bear   112
With hounds of Sparta. Never did I hear   113
Such gallant chiding; for, besides the groves,   114
The skies, the fountains, every region near
Seemed all one mutual cry. I never heard
So musical a discord, such sweet thunder.

THESEUS

My hounds are bred out of the Spartan kind,   118
So flewed, so sanded; and their heads are hung   119
With ears that sweep away the morning dew;
Crook-kneed, and dewlapped like Thessalian bulls;   121
Slow in pursuit, but matched in mouth like bells,   122
Each under each. A cry more tunable   123
Was never holloed to, nor cheered with horn,   124
In Crete, in Sparta, nor in Thessaly.
Judge when you hear. [*He sees the sleepers.*] But, soft!
  What nymphs are these?

EGEUS

My lord, this is my daughter here asleep,
And this Lysander; this Demetrius is,
This Helena, old Nedar's Helena.
I wonder of their being here together.   130

THESEUS

No doubt they rose up early to observe

---

106 Uncouple set free for the hunt   **111 Cadmus** mythical founder of
Thebes. (This story about him is unknown.)   **112 bayed** brought to
bay   **113 hounds of Sparta** (A breed famous in antiquity for their
hunting skill.)   **114 chiding** i.e., yelping   **118 kind** strain, breed   **119 So
flewed** similarly having large hanging chaps or fleshy covering of the
jaw.   **sanded** of sandy color   **121 dewlapped** having pendulous folds of
skin under the neck   **122–123 matched . . . each** i.e., harmoniously
matched in their various cries like a set of bells, from treble down to
bass   **123 cry** pack of hounds.   **tunable** well tuned, melodious
124 cheered encouraged   **130 wonder of** wonder at

The rite of May, and hearing our intent,
Came here in grace of our solemnity.   133
But speak, Egeus. Is not this the day
That Hermia should give answer of her choice?

EGEUS   It is, my lord.

THESEUS
Go, bid the huntsmen wake them with their horns.
                              [*Exit an Attendant.*]

Shout within. Wind horns. They all start up.

Good morrow, friends. Saint Valentine is past.   138
Begin these woodbirds but to couple now?

LYSANDER
Pardon, my lord.   [*They kneel.*]

THESEUS   I pray you all, stand up.
I know you two are rival enemies;
How comes this gentle concord in the world,
That hatred is so far from jealousy   143
To sleep by hate and fear no enmity?

LYSANDER
My lord, I shall reply amazedly,
Half sleep, half waking; but as yet, I swear,
I cannot truly say how I came here.
But, as I think—for truly would I speak,
And now I do bethink me, so it is—
I came with Hermia hither. Our intent
Was to be gone from Athens, where we might,   151
Without the peril of the Athenian law—   152

EGEUS
Enough, enough, my lord; you have enough.
I beg the law, the law, upon his head.
They would have stol'n away; they would, Demetrius,
Thereby to have defeated you and me,   156
You of your wife and me of my consent,
Of my consent that she should be your wife.

DEMETRIUS
My lord, fair Helen told me of their stealth,

133 in . . . solemnity in honor of our wedding   **138 Saint Valentine**
(Birds were supposed to choose their mates on Saint Valentine's Day.)
143 jealousy suspicion   **151 where** wherever; or, to where   **152 Without**
outside of, beyond   **156 defeated** defrauded

Of this their purpose hither to this wood,   160
And I in fury hither followed them,
Fair Helena in fancy following me.
But, my good lord, I wot not by what power—
But by some power it is—my love to Hermia,
Melted as the snow, seems to me now
As the remembrance of an idle gaud   166
Which in my childhood I did dote upon;
And all the faith, the virtue of my heart,
The object and the pleasure of mine eye,
Is only Helena. To her, my lord,
Was I betrothed ere I saw Hermia,
But like a sickness did I loathe this food;
But, as in health, come to my natural taste,
Now I do wish it, love it, long for it,
And will for evermore be true to it.

THESEUS
Fair lovers, you are fortunately met.
Of this discourse we more will hear anon.
Egeus, I will overbear your will;
For in the temple, by and by, with us
These couples shall eternally be knit.
And, for the morning now is something worn,   181
Our purposed hunting shall be set aside.
Away with us to Athens. Three and three,
We'll hold a feast in great solemnity.
Come, Hippolyta.
          [*Exeunt Theseus, Hippolyta, Egeus, and train.*]

DEMETRIUS
These things seem small and undistinguishable,
Like far-off mountains turnèd into clouds.

HERMIA
Methinks I see these things with parted eye,   188
When everything seems double.

HELENA   So methinks;
And I have found Demetrius like a jewel,   190
Mine own, and not mine own.

DEMETRIUS   Are you sure   191

160 hither in coming hither   **166 idle gaud** worthless trinket   **181 for**
since.   **something** somewhat   **188 parted** improperly focused
190–191 like . . . mine own i.e., like a jewel that one finds by chance and
therefore possesses but cannot certainly consider one's own property

That we are awake? It seems to me
That yet we sleep, we dream. Do not you think
The Duke was here, and bid us follow him?

HERMIA
Yea, and my father.

HELENA   And Hippolyta.

LYSANDER
And he did bid us follow to the temple.

DEMETRIUS
Why, then, we are awake. Let's follow him,
And by the way let us recount our dreams.   [*Exeunt.*]

BOTTOM [*Awaking*] When my cue comes, call me, and
I will answer. My next is, "Most fair Pyramus." Heigh-
ho! Peter Quince! Flute, the bellows mender! Snout,
the tinker! Starveling! God's my life, stolen hence and   202
left me asleep! I have had a most rare vision. I have
had a dream, past the wit of man to say what dream it
was. Man is but an ass if he go about to expound this   205
dream. Methought I was—there is no man can tell
what. Methought I was—and methought I had—but
man is but a patched fool if he will offer to say what   208
methought I had. The eye of man hath not heard, the   209
ear of man hath not seen, man's hand is not able to
taste, his tongue to conceive, nor his heart to report,   211
what my dream was. I will get Peter Quince to write
a ballad of this dream. It shall be called "Bottom's
Dream," because it hath no bottom; and I will sing it
in the latter end of a play, before the Duke. Peradven-
ture, to make it the more gracious, I shall sing it at her   216
death.   [*Exit.*]

❖

4.2   *Enter Quince, Flute, [Snout, and Starveling].*

QUINCE   Have you sent to Bottom's house? Is he come
home yet?

202 God's may God save   **205 go about** attempt   **208 patched** wearing
motley, i.e., a dress of various colors.   **offer** venture   **209–211 The eye
. . . report** (Bottom garbles the terms of 1 Corinthians 2:9.)   **216 her**
Thisbe's (?)

4.2. Location: Athens.

STARVELING   He cannot be heard of. Out of doubt he is
transported.   4

FLUTE   If he come not, then the play is marred. It goes
not forward, doth it?

QUINCE   It is not possible. You have not a man in all
Athens able to _discharge_ Pyramus but he.   8

FLUTE   No, he hath simply the best _wit_ of any handicraft 9
man in Athens.

QUINCE   Yea, and the best _person_ too, and he is a very 11
paramour for a sweet voice.

FLUTE   You must say "paragon." A paramour is, God
bless us, _a thing of naught._   14

   Enter Snug the joiner.

SNUG   Masters, the Duke is coming from the temple,
and there is two or three lords and ladies more married. If our sport had gone forward, _we had all been_ 17
made men.   18

FLUTE   O sweet bully Bottom! Thus hath he lost _six-_ 19
pence a day during his life; he could not have scaped 20
sixpence a day. An the Duke had not given him sixpence a day for playing Pyramus, I'll be hanged. He
would have deserved it. Sixpence a day in Pyramus, or
nothing.

   Enter Bottom.

BOTTOM   Where are these lads? Where are these _hearts?_ 25

QUINCE   Bottom! O most courageous day! O most
happy hour!

BOTTOM   Masters, _I am to discourse wonders._ But ask 28
me not what; for if I tell you, I am no true Athenian. I
will tell you everything, right as it fell out.

QUINCE   Let us hear, sweet Bottom.

BOTTOM   Not a word _of me._ All that I will tell you is— 32
that the Duke hath dined. Get your apparel together,

4 transported carried off by fairies; or, possibly, transformed
8 discharge perform   **9 wit** intellect   **11 person** appearance   **14 a . . .
naught** a shameful thing   **17–18 we . . . men** i.e., we would have had our
fortunes made   **19–20 sixpence a day** i.e., as a royal pension   **25 hearts**
good fellows   **28 am . . . wonders** have wonders to relate   **32 of** out of

good strings to your beards, new ribbons to your 34
pumps; meet presently at the palace; every man look 35
o'er his part; for the short and the long is, our play is
preferred. In any case, let Thisbe have clean linen; and 37
let not him that plays the lion pare his nails, for they
shall hang out for the lion's claws. And, most dear actors, eat no onions nor garlic, for we are to utter sweet
breath; and I do not doubt but to hear them say it is
a sweet comedy. No more words. Away! Go, away!
                                          [*Exeunt.*]

❖

34 strings (to attach the beards)   **35 pumps** light shoes or slippers.
presently immediately   **37 preferred** selected for consideration

5.1 *Enter Theseus, Hippolyta, and Philostrate,*
[lords, and attendants].

HIPPOLYTA
  'Tis strange, my Theseus, that these lovers speak of.   1
THESEUS
  More strange than true. I never may believe   2
  These antique fables nor these fairy toys.   3
  Lovers and madmen have such seething brains,
  Such shaping fantasies, that apprehend   5
  More than cool reason ever comprehends.   6
  The lunatic, the lover, and the poet
  Are of imagination all compact.   8
  One sees more devils than vast hell can hold;
  That is the madman. The lover, all as frantic,
  Sees Helen's beauty in a brow of Egypt.   11
  The poet's eye, in a fine frenzy rolling,
  Doth glance from heaven to earth, from earth to heaven;
  And as imagination bodies forth
  The forms of things unknown, the poet's pen
  Turns them to shapes and gives to airy nothing
  A local habitation and a name.
  Such tricks hath strong imagination
  That, if it would but apprehend some joy,
  It comprehends some bringer of that joy;   20
  Or in the night, imagining some fear,   21
  How easy is a bush supposed a bear!
HIPPOLYTA
  But all the story of the night told over,
  And all their minds transfigured so together,
  More witnesseth than fancy's images   25
  And grows to something of great constancy;   26
  But, howsoever, strange and admirable.   27

5.1. Location: Athens. The palace of Theseus.
1 that that which **2 may** can **3 antique** old-fashioned (punning too on
antic, strange, grotesque). **fairy toys** trifling stories about fairies
5 fantasies imaginations. **apprehend** conceive, imagine **6 comprehends** understands **8 compact** formed, composed **11 Helen's** i.e., of
Helen of Troy, pattern of beauty. **brow of Egypt** i.e., face of a gypsy
20 bringer i.e., source **21 fear** object of fear **25 More . . . images** testi-
fies to something more substantial than mere imaginings **26 constancy**
certainty **27 howsoever** in any case. **admirable** a source of wonder

*Enter lovers: Lysander, Demetrius, Hermia, and
Helena.*

THESEUS
  Here come the lovers, full of joy and mirth.
  Joy, gentle friends! Joy and fresh days of love
  Accompany your hearts!
LYSANDER   More than to us
  Wait in your royal walks, your board, your bed!
THESEUS
  Come now, what masques, what dances shall we have   32
  To wear away this long age of three hours
  Between our after-supper and bedtime?
  Where is our usual manager of mirth?
  What revels are in hand? Is there no play
  To ease the anguish of a torturing hour?
  Call Philostrate.
PHILOSTRATE   Here, mighty Theseus.
THESEUS
  Say what abridgment have you for this evening?   39
  What masque? What music? How shall we beguile
  The lazy time, if not with some delight?
PHILOSTRATE [*Giving him a paper*]
  There is a brief how many sports are ripe.   42
  Make choice of which Your Highness will see first.
THESEUS [*Reads*]
  "The battle with the Centaurs, to be sung   44
  By an Athenian eunuch to the harp"?
  We'll none of that. That have I told my love,
  In glory of my kinsman Hercules.   47
  [*Reads.*] "The riot of the tipsy Bacchanals,   48
  Tearing the Thracian singer in their rage"?   49
  That is an old device; and it was played   50

___

32 masques courtly entertainments   **39 abridgment** pastime (to abridge
or shorten the evening)   **42 brief** short written statement, summary
44 battle . . . Centaurs (Probably refers to the battle of the Centaurs and
the Lapithae, when the Centaurs attempted to carry off Hippodamia,
bride of Theseus' friend Pirothous.)   **47 kinsman** (Plutarch's "Life of
Theseus" states that Hercules and Theseus were near kinsmen. Theseus
is referring to a version of the battle of the Centaurs in which Hercules
was said to be present.)   **48–49 The riot . . . rage** (This was the story of
the death of Orpheus, as told in *Metamorphoses* 9.)   **50 device** show,
performance

When I from Thebes came last a conqueror.
[*Reads.*] "The thrice three Muses mourning for the
  death   52
Of Learning, late deceased in beggary"?   53
That is some satire, keen and critical,
Not sorting with a nuptial ceremony.   55
[*Reads.*] "A tedious brief scene of young Pyramus
And his love Thisbe; very tragical mirth"?
Merry and tragical? Tedious and brief?
That is hot ice and wondrous strange snow.   59
How shall we find the concord of this discord?
PHILOSTRATE
A play there is, my lord, some ten words long,
Which is as brief as I have known a play;
But by ten words, my lord, it is too long,
Which makes it tedious. For in all the play
There is not one word apt, one player fitted.
And tragical, my noble lord, it is,
For Pyramus therein doth kill himself.
Which, when I saw rehearsed, I must confess,
Made mine eyes water; but more merry tears
The passion of loud laughter never shed.
THESEUS   What are they that do play it?
PHILOSTRATE
Hard-handed men that work in Athens here,
Which never labored in their minds till now,
And now have toiled their unbreathed memories   74
With this same play, against your nuptial.   75
THESEUS   And we will hear it.
PHILOSTRATE   No, my noble lord,
It is not for you. I have heard it over,
And it is nothing, nothing in the world;
Unless you can find sport in their intents,
Extremely stretched and conned with cruel pain   80
To do you service.
THESEUS   I will hear that play;

52–53 The thrice . . . beggary (Possibly an allusion to Spenser's *Teares of the Muses*, 1591, though "satires" deploring the neglect of learning and the creative arts were commonplace.) **55 sorting with** befitting **59 strange** (Sometimes emended to an adjective that would contrast with *snow*, just as *hot* contrasts with *ice*.) **74 toiled** taxed. **unbreathed** unexercised **75 against** in preparation for **80 stretched** strained. **conned** memorized

For never anything can be amiss
When <u>simpleness</u> and duty tender it.   83
Go bring them in; and take your places, ladies.
               [*Philostrate goes to summon the players.*]

HIPPOLYTA
I love not to see <u>wretchedness o'ercharged</u>,   85
And duty in <u>his service</u> perishing.   86

THESEUS
Why, gentle sweet, you shall see no such thing.

HIPPOLYTA
He says they can do nothing in this <u>kind.</u>   88

THESEUS
The kinder we, to give them thanks for nothing.
Our sport shall be to take what they mistake;
And what poor duty cannot do, noble <u>respect</u>   91
<u>Takes it in might, not merit.</u>   92
Where I have come, great <u>clerks</u> have purposèd   93
To greet me with premeditated welcomes;
Where I have seen them shiver and look pale,
Make periods in the midst of sentences,
Throttle their <u>practiced accent</u> in their fears,   97
And in conclusion dumbly have broke off,
Not paying me a welcome. Trust me, sweet,
Out of this silence yet I picked a welcome;
And in the modesty of fearful duty
I read as much as from the rattling tongue
Of saucy and audacious eloquence.
Love, therefore, and tongue-tied simplicity
In <u>least</u> speak most, to <u>my capacity.</u>   105

     [*Philostrate returns.*]

PHILOSTRATE
So please Your Grace, the <u>Prologue is addressed.</u>   106
THESEUS   Let him approach.   [*A flourish of trumpets.*]

---

83 simpleness simplicity   **85 wretchedness o'ercharged** incompetence
overburdened   **86 his service** its attempt to serve   **88 kind** kind of thing
91 respect evaluation, consideration   **92 Takes . . . merit** values it
for the effort made rather than for the excellence achieved   **93 clerks**
learned men   **97 practiced accent** i.e., rehearsed speech; or, usual way of
speaking   **105 least** i.e., saying least.   **to my capacity** in my judgment
and understanding   **106 Prologue** speaker of the prologue.   **addressed**
ready

Enter the Prologue [Quince].

PROLOGUE
If we offend, it is with our good will.
  That you should think, we come not to offend,
But with good will. To show our simple skill,
  That is the true beginning of our end.
Consider then, we come but in despite.
  We do not come, as minding to content you,   113
Our true intent is. All for your delight
  We are not here. That you should here repent you,
The actors are at hand; and, by their show,
You shall know all that you are like to know.

THESEUS   This fellow doth not stand upon points.   118
LYSANDER   He hath rid his prologue like a rough colt;   119
he knows not the stop. A good moral, my lord: it is not   120
enough to speak, but to speak true.

HIPPOLYTA   Indeed he hath played on his prologue like
a child on a recorder; a sound, but not in government.   123

THESEUS   His speech was like a tangled chain: nothing   124
impaired, but all disordered. Who is next?

Enter Pyramus [Bottom] and Thisbe [Flute], and
Wall [Snout], and Moonshine [Starveling], and
Lion [Snug].

PROLOGUE
Gentles, perchance you wonder at this show;
  But wonder on, till truth make all things plain.
This man is Pyramus, if you would know;
  This beauteous lady Thisbe is certain.
This man with lime and roughcast doth present
  Wall, that vile Wall which did these lovers sunder;
And through Wall's chink, poor souls, they are content
  To whisper. At the which let no man wonder.
This man, with lantern, dog, and bush of thorn,
  Presenteth Moonshine; for, if you will know,

---

113 minding intending   **118 stand upon points** (1) heed niceties or small
points (2) pay attention to punctuation in his reading. (The humor of
Quince's speech is in the blunders of its punctuation.)   **119 rid** ridden.
rough unbroken   **120 stop** (1) the stopping of a colt by reining it in
(2) punctuation mark   **123 recorder** a wind instrument like a flute or fla-
geolet.   **government** control   **124 nothing** not at all

By moonshine did these lovers think no scorn   136
  To meet at Ninus' tomb, there, there to woo.
This grisly beast, which Lion hight by name,   138
The trusty Thisbe coming first by night
Did scare away, or rather did affright;
And as she fled, her mantle she did fall,   141
  Which Lion vile with bloody mouth did stain.
Anon comes Pyramus, sweet youth and tall,   143
  And finds his trusty Thisbe's mantle slain;
Whereat, with blade, with bloody blameful blade,
  He bravely broached his boiling bloody breast.   146
And Thisbe, tarrying in mulberry shade,
  His dagger drew, and died. For all the rest,
Let Lion, Moonshine, Wall, and lovers twain
  At large discourse while here they do remain.   150
          Exeunt Lion, Thisbe, and Moonshine.
THESEUS I wonder if the lion be to speak.
DEMETRIUS No wonder, my lord. One lion may, when
  many asses do.
WALL
In this same interlude it doth befall   154
That I, one Snout by name, present a wall;
And such a wall as I would have you think
That had in it a crannied hole or chink,
Through which the lovers, Pyramus and Thisbe,
Did whisper often, very secretly.
This loam, this roughcast, and this stone doth show
That I am that same wall; the truth is so.
And this the cranny is, right and sinister,   162
Through which the fearful lovers are to whisper.
THESEUS Would you desire lime and hair to speak
  better?
DEMETRIUS It is the wittiest partition that ever I heard   166
  discourse, my lord.

          [*Pyramus comes forward.*]

136 **think no scorn** think it no disgraceful matter 138 **hight** is called
141 **fall** let fall 143 **tall** courageous 146 **broached** stabbed 150 **At large**
in full, at length 154 **interlude** play 162 **right and sinister** i.e., the right
side of it and the left; or, running from right to left, horizontally 166 **partition** (1) wall (2) section of a learned treatise or oration

THESEUS   Pyramus draws near the wall. Silence!

PYRAMUS

O grim-looked night! O night with hue so black!   169
  O night, which ever art when day is not!
O night, O night! Alack, alack, alack,
  I fear my Thisbe's promise is forgot.
And thou, O wall, O sweet, O lovely wall,
  That stand'st between her father's ground and mine,
Thou wall, O wall, O sweet and lovely wall,
  Show me thy chink, to blink through with mine eyne!
          [*Wall makes a chink with his fingers.*]
Thanks, courteous wall. Jove shield thee well for this.
  But what see I? No Thisbe do I see.
O wicked wall, through whom I see no bliss!
  Cursed be thy stones for thus deceiving me!

THESEUS   The wall, methinks, being <u>sensible,</u> should   181
curse again.

PYRAMUS   No, in truth, sir, he should not. "Deceiving
me" is Thisbe's cue: she is to enter now, and I am to
spy her through the wall. You shall see, it will fall <u>pat</u>   185
as I told you. Yonder she comes.

          Enter Thisbe.

THISBE

O wall, full often hast thou heard my moans,
  For parting my fair Pyramus and me.
My cherry lips have often kissed thy stones,
  Thy stones with lime and hair knit up in thee.

PYRAMUS

I see a voice. Now will I to the chink,
  To spy <u>an</u> I can hear my Thisbe's face.   192
Thisbe!

THISBE   My love! Thou art my love, I think.

PYRAMUS

  Think what thou wilt, I am thy <u>lover's grace,</u>   194
And like <u>Limander</u> am I trusty still.   195

THISBE

And I like <u>Helen,</u> till the Fates me kill.   196

---

169 grim-looked grim-looking   **181 sensible** capable of feeling   **185 pat**
exactly   **192 an** if   **194 lover's grace** i.e., gracious lover   **195, 196 Liman-
der, Helen** (Blunders for *Leander* and *Hero*.)

PYRAMUS
  Not Shafalus to Procrus was so true.   197
THISBE
  As Shafalus to Procrus, I to you.
PYRAMUS
  O, kiss me through the hole of this vile wall!
THISBE
  I kiss the wall's hole, not your lips at all.
PYRAMUS
  Wilt thou at Ninny's tomb meet me straightway?
THISBE
  'Tide life, 'tide death, I come without delay.   202
                    [*Exeunt Pyramus and Thisbe.*]
WALL
  Thus have I, Wall, my part dischargèd so;
  And, being done, thus Wall away doth go.   [*Exit.*]
THESEUS Now is the mural down between the two
  neighbors.
DEMETRIUS No remedy, my lord, when walls are so
  willful to hear without warning.   208
HIPPOLYTA This is the silliest stuff that ever I heard.
THESEUS The best in this kind are but shadows; and the   210
  worst are no worse, if imagination amend them.
HIPPOLYTA It must be your imagination then, and not
  theirs.
THESEUS If we imagine no worse of them than they of
  themselves, they may pass for excellent men. Here
  come two noble beasts in, a man and a lion.

        Enter Lion and Moonshine.

LION
  You, ladies, you whose gentle hearts do fear
    The smallest monstrous mouse that creeps on floor,
  May now perchance both quake and tremble here,
    When lion rough in wildest rage doth roar.
  Then know that I, as Snug the joiner, am

197 **Shafalus, Procrus** (Blunders for *Cephalus* and *Procris,* also famous
lovers.) 202 **'Tide** betide, come 208 **willful** willing. **without warning**
i.e., without warning the parents. (Demetrius makes a joke on the proverb
"Walls have ears.") 210 **in this kind** of this sort. **shadows** likenesses,
representations

A lion fell, nor else no lion's dam;   222
For, if I should as lion come in strife
Into this place, 'twere pity on my life.

THESEUS A very gentle beast, and of a good conscience.

DEMETRIUS The very best at a beast, my lord, that e'er
I saw.

LYSANDER This lion is a very fox for his valor.   228

THESEUS True; and a goose for his discretion.   229

DEMETRIUS Not so, my lord; for his valor cannot carry
his discretion; and the fox carries the goose.

THESEUS His discretion, I am sure, cannot carry his
valor; for the goose carries not the fox. It is well. Leave
it to his discretion, and let us listen to the moon.

MOON
This lanthorn doth the hornèd moon present—   235

DEMETRIUS He should have worn the horns on his 236
head.   237

THESEUS He is no crescent, and his horns are invisible
within the circumference.

MOON
This lanthorn doth the hornèd moon present;
Myself the man i' the moon do seem to be.

THESEUS This is the greatest error of all the rest. The
man should be put into the lanthorn. How is it else
the man i' the moon?

DEMETRIUS He dares not come there for the candle, for 245
you see, it is already in snuff.   246

HIPPOLYTA I am aweary of this moon. Would he would
change!

THESEUS It appears, by his small light of discretion, that
he is in the wane; but yet, in courtesy, in all reason,
we must stay the time.

---

222 lion fell fierce lion (with a play on the idea of "lion skin") **228 is . . .
valor** i.e., his valor consists of craftiness and discretion   **229 goose . . .
discretion** i.e., as discreet as a goose, that is, more foolish than discreet
235 lanthorn (This original spelling, *lanthorn*, may suggest a play on the
horn of which lanterns were made, and also on a cuckold's horns; but the
spelling *lanthorn* is not used consistently for comic effect in this play or
elsewhere. At 5.1.134, for example, the word is *lantern* in the original.)
236–237 on his head (as a sign of cuckoldry)   **245 for the** because of the
246 in snuff (1) offended (2) in need of snuffing or trimming

LYSANDER   Proceed, Moon.

MOON   All that I have to say is to tell you that the lanthorn is the moon, I, the man i' the moon, this thornbush my thornbush, and this dog my dog.

DEMETRIUS   Why, all these should be in the lanthorn,
for all these are in the moon. But silence! Here comes
Thisbe.

Enter Thisbe.

THISBE
This is old Ninny's tomb. Where is my love?

LION [*Roaring*]   O!

DEMETRIUS   Well roared, Lion.

[*Thisbe runs off, dropping her mantle.*]

THESEUS   Well run, Thisbe.

HIPPOLYTA   Well shone, Moon. Truly, the moon shines
with a good grace.

[*The Lion worries Thisbe's mantle.*]

THESEUS   Well moused, Lion.   265

Enter Pyramus.   [*Exit Lion.*]

DEMETRIUS   And then came Pyramus.

LYSANDER   And so the lion vanished.

PYRAMUS
Sweet Moon, I thank thee for thy sunny beams;
   I thank thee, Moon, for shining now so bright;
For, by thy gracious, golden, glittering gleams,
   I trust to take of truest Thisbe sight.
      But stay, O spite!
      But mark, poor knight,
What dreadful dole is here?   274
      Eyes, do you see?
      How can it be?
O dainty duck! O dear!
      Thy mantle good,
      What, stained with blood!
Approach, ye Furies fell!   280
      O Fates, come, come,   281

---

265 moused shaken, torn, bitten   **274 dole** grievous event   **280 Furies**
avenging goddesses of Greek myth.   **fell** fierce   **281 Fates** the three
goddesses (Clotho, Lachesis, Atropos) of Greek myth who drew and cut
the thread of human life

       Cut thread and thrum;   282
        Quail, crush, conclude, and quell!   283

THESEUS   This passion, and the death of a dear friend,   284
would go near to make a man look sad.   285

HIPPOLYTA   Beshrew my heart, but I pity the man.

PYRAMUS
   O, wherefore, Nature, didst thou lions frame?
   Since lion vile hath here deflowered my dear,
   Which is—no, no, which was—the fairest dame
   That lived, that loved, that liked, that looked with cheer.   290
      Come, tears, confound,
      Out, sword, and wound
     The pap of Pyramus;   293
       Ay, that left pap,
       Where heart doth hop.   [*He stabs himself.*]
   Thus die I, thus, thus, thus.
      Now am I dead,
      Now am I fled;
   My soul is in the sky.
      Tongue, lose thy light;
      Moon, take thy flight.   [*Exit Moonshine.*]
    Now die, die, die, die, die.   [*Pyramus dies.*]

DEMETRIUS   No die, but an ace, for him; for he is   303
but one.   304

LYSANDER   Less than an ace, man; for he is dead, he is
nothing.

THESEUS   With the help of a surgeon he might yet re-
cover, and yet prove an ass.   308

HIPPOLYTA   How chance Moonshine is gone before
Thisbe comes back and finds her lover?

THESEUS   She will find him by starlight.

     [*Enter Thisbe.*]

Here she comes, and her passion ends the play.

---

282 thread and thrum the warp in weaving and the loose end of the
warp   **283 Quail** overpower.   **quell** kill, destroy   **284–285 This . . . sad**
i.e., if one had other reason to grieve, one might be sad, but not from this
absurd portrayal of passion   **290 cheer** countenance   **293 pap** breast
303 ace the side of the die featuring the single pip, or spot. (The pun is on
die as a singular of *dice*; Bottom's performance is not worth a whole *die*
but rather one single face of it, one small portion.)   **304 one** (1) an individ-
ual person (2) unique   **308 ass** (with a pun on *ace*)

HIPPOLYTA   Methinks she should not use a long one for
such a Pyramus. I hope she will be brief.

DEMETRIUS   A mote will turn the balance, which Pyra-   315
mus, which Thisbe, is the better: he for a man, God   316
warrant us; she for a woman, God bless us.

LYSANDER   She hath spied him already with those sweet
eyes.

DEMETRIUS   And thus she means, videlicet: 320

THISBE
   Asleep, my love?
   What, dead, my dove?
  O Pyramus, arise!
   Speak, speak. Quite dumb?
   Dead, dead? A tomb
  Must cover thy sweet eyes.
   These lily lips,
   This cherry nose,
  These yellow cowslip cheeks,
   Are gone, are gone!
   Lovers, make moan.
  His eyes were green as leeks.
   O Sisters Three,   333
   Come, come to me,
  With hands as pale as milk;
   Lay them in gore,
   Since you have shore   337
  With shears his thread of silk.
   Tongue, not a word.
   Come, trusty sword,
  Come, blade, my breast imbrue! [*Stabs herself.*]   341
   And farewell, friends.
   Thus Thisbe ends.
  Adieu, adieu, adieu.   [*She dies.*]

THESEUS   Moonshine and Lion are left to bury the dead.

DEMETRIUS   Ay, and Wall too.

BOTTOM [*Starting up, as Flute does also*]   No, I assure you,
the wall is down that parted their fathers. Will it

---

315 mote small particle **315–316 which ... which** whether ... or
320 means moans, laments. **videlicet** to wit **333 Sisters Three** the
Fates **337 shore** shorn **341 imbrue** stain with blood

please you to see the epilogue, or to hear a <u>Bergomask</u> 349
<u>dance</u> between two of our company? 350

                              [*The other players enter.*]

THESEUS No epilogue, I pray you; for your play needs
no excuse. Never excuse; for when the players are all
dead, there need none to be blamed. Marry, if he that
writ it had played Pyramus and hanged himself in
Thisbe's garter, it would have been a fine tragedy; and
so it is, truly, and very notably discharged. But, come,
your Bergomask. Let your epilogue alone.   [*A dance.*]
The <u>iron tongue</u> of midnight hath <u>told</u> twelve. 358
Lovers, to bed, 'tis almost fairy time.
I fear we shall outsleep the coming morn
As much as we this night have <u>overwatched</u>. 361
This <u>palpable-gross</u> play hath well beguiled 362
The <u>heavy</u> gait of night. Sweet friends, to bed. 363
A fortnight hold we this solemnity,
In nightly revels and new jollity.   *Exeunt.*

   Enter Puck [*carrying a broom*].

PUCK

    Now the hungry lion roars,
      And the wolf behowls the moon;
    Whilst the <u>heavy</u> plowman snores, 368
      All with weary task <u>fordone.</u> 369
    Now the <u>wasted brands</u> do glow, 370
      Whilst the screech owl, screeching loud,
    Puts the wretch that lies in woe
      In remembrance of a shroud.
    Now it is the time of night
      That the graves, all gaping wide,
    <u>Every one lets forth his sprite,</u> 376
      In the church-way paths to glide.
    And we fairies, that do run

349–350 Bergomask dance a rustic dance named from Bergamo, a province in the state of Venice **358 iron tongue** i.e., of a bell. **told** counted, struck ("tolled") **361 overwatched** stayed up too late **362 palpable-gross** palpably gross, obviously crude **363 heavy** drowsy, dull **368 heavy** tired **369 fordone** exhausted **370 wasted brands** burned-out logs **376 Every . . . sprite** every grave lets forth its ghost

By the triple Hecate's team   379
From the presence of the sun,
   Following darkness like a dream,
Now are frolic. Not a mouse   382
Shall disturb this hallowed house.
I am sent with broom before,
To sweep the dust behind the door.   385

*Enter [Oberon and Titania,] King and Queen of
Fairies, with all their train.*

OBERON
Through the house give glimmering light,
   By the dead and drowsy fire;
Every elf and fairy sprite
   Hop as light as bird from brier;
And this ditty, after me,
Sing, and dance it trippingly.

TITANIA
First, rehearse your song by rote,
To each word a warbling note.
Hand in hand, with fairy grace,
Will we sing, and bless this place.
                    [Song and dance.]

OBERON
Now, until the break of day,
Through this house each fairy stray.
To the best bride-bed will we,
Which by us shall blessèd be;
And the issue there create   400
Ever shall be fortunate.
So shall all the couples three
Ever true in loving be;
And the blots of Nature's hand
Shall not in their issue stand;
Never mole, harelip, nor scar,
Nor mark prodigious, such as are   407
Despisèd in nativity,

379 triple Hecate's (Hecate ruled in three capacities: as Luna or Cynthia
in heaven, as Diana on earth, and as Proserpina in hell.)   **382 frolic**
merry   **385 behind** from behind. (Robin Goodfellow was a household
spirit who helped good housemaids and punished lazy ones.)   **400 create**
created   **407 prodigious** monstrous, unnatural

Shall upon their children be.
With this field dew consecrate   410
Every fairy take his gait,   411
And each several chamber bless,   412
Through this palace, with sweet peace;
And the owner of it blest
Ever shall in safety rest.
Trip away; make no stay;
Meet me all by break of day.

    Exeunt [*Oberon, Titania, and train*].

PUCK [*To the audience*]
If we shadows have offended,
Think but this, and all is mended,
That you have but slumbered here   420
While these visions did appear.
And this weak and idle theme,
No more yielding but a dream,   423
Gentles, do not reprehend.
If you pardon, we will mend.   425
And, as I am an honest Puck,
If we have unearnèd luck
Now to scape the serpent's tongue,   428
We will make amends ere long;
Else the Puck a liar call.
So, good night unto you all.
Give me your hands, if we be friends,   432
And Robin shall restore amends.   [*Exit.*] 433

---

410 consecrate consecrated **411 take his gait** go his way **412 several** separate **420 That . . . here** i.e., that it is a "midsummer night's dream" **423 No . . . but** yielding no more than **425 mend** improve **428 serpent's tongue** i.e., hissing **432 Give . . . hands** applaud **433 restore amends** give satisfaction in return

Date and Text

A Midsummer Night's Dream was entered on the Stationers' Register, the official record book of the London Company of Stationers (booksellers and printers), by Thomas Fisher on October 8, 1600, and printed by him that same year in quarto:

> A Midsommer nights dreame. As it hath beene sundry times pub*lickely acted, by the Right honoura*ble, the Lord Chamberlaine his *seruants. Written by William Shakespeare.* Imprinted at London, for *Thomas Fisher*, and are to be soulde at his shoppe, at the Signe of the White Hart, in *Fleetestreete*. 1600.

This text appears to have been set from Shakespeare's working manuscript. Its inconsistencies in time scheme and other irregularities may reflect some revision, although the inconsistencies are not noticeable in performance. A second quarto appeared in 1619, though falsely dated 1600; it was a reprint of the first quarto, with some minor corrections and many new errors. A copy of this second quarto, evidently with some added stage directions and other minor changes from a theatrical manuscript in the company's possession, served as the basis for the First Folio text of 1623. Essentially, the first quarto remains the authoritative text.

Other than Francis Meres's listing of the play in 1598 in his *Palladis Tamia: Wit's Treasury* (a slender volume on contemporary literature and art; valuable because it lists most of the plays of Shakespeare's that existed at that time), external clues as to date are elusive. The description of unruly weather (2.1.88–114) has been related to the bad summer of 1594, but complaints about the weather are perennial. On the assumption that the play celebrates some noble wedding of the period, scholars have come up with a number of suitable marriages. Chief are those of Sir Thomas Heneage to Mary, Countess of Southampton, in 1594; of William Stanley, Earl of Derby, to Elizabeth Vere, daughter of the Earl of Oxford, in 1595; and of Thomas, son of Lord Berkeley, to Elizabeth, daughter of Lord Carey, in 1596. The Countess of Southampton was the widowed mother of the young Earl of Southampton, to whom Shakespeare had dedicated his *Venus and Adonis* and *The Rape of Lucrece*. No one has ever proved convincingly, however, that the play was written for any occasion other than commercial public performance. The play makes sense for a general audience and does not need to depend on references to a private marriage. Shakespeare was, after all, in the business of writing plays for his fellow actors, who earned their livelihood chiefly by public acting before large paying audiences. In any event the search for a court marriage is a circular argument in terms of dating; suitable court marriages can be found for any year of the decade. In the last analysis, the play has to be dated on the basis of its stylistic affinity to plays like *Romeo and Juliet* and *Richard II*, works of the "lyric" mid 1590s. The "Pyramus and Thisbe" performance in *A Midsummer Night's Dream* would seem to bear an obvious relation to *Romeo and Juliet*, although no one can say for sure which came first.

Textual Notes

These textual notes are not an historical collation, either of the early quartos and the early folios or of more recent editions; they are simply a record of departures in this edition from the copy text. The reading adopted in this edition appears in boldface, followed by the rejected reading from the copy text, i.e., the quarto of 1600. Only major alterations in punctuation are noted. Changes in lineation are not indicated, nor are some minor and obvious typographical errors.

Abbreviations used:
Q the first quarto of 1600
s.d. stage direction
s.p. speech prefix

Copy text: the first quarto of 1600.

1.1. 4 wanes waues **10 New bent** Now bent **19 s.d. Lysander** Lysander and Helena **24 Stand forth, Demetrius** [printed as s.d. in Q] **26 Stand forth, Lysander** [printed as s.d. in Q] **74 their** there **132 Ay** Eigh **136 low** loue **187 Yours would** Your words **191 I'd** ile **216 sweet** sweld **219 stranger companies** strange companions

2.1. 1 s.p. [and elsewhere] Puck Robin **61 s.p. [and elsewhere] Titania** Qu **61 Fairies** Fairy **69 step** steppe **79 Aegles** Eagles **109 thin** chinne **158 the west** west **190 slay** stay. **slayeth** stayeth **194 thee** the **201 not nor** not not **246 s.d.** [at l. 247 in Q]

2.2. 9 s.p. First Fairy [not in Q; also at l. 20] **13 s.p. Chorus** [not in Q; also at l. 24] **45 Be it** Bet it **49 good** god **53 is** it

3.1. 27–28 yourselves your selfe **52 s.p. Bottom** Cet **72 s.p. Puck** Ro **77 s.p. Bottom** Pyra [also at ll. 79 and 98] **78 Odors, odors** Odours, odorous **83 s.p. Puck** Quin **84 s.p. Flute** Thys [also at ll. 88 and 97] **144 own** owe **157–158 Ready . . . go** [assigned to Fairies in Q] **170 s.p. Peaseblossom** 1. Fai **171 Hail** [assigned in Q to 1. Fai] **172 s.p. Mote** 2. Fair **173 s.p. Mustardseed** 3. Fai **190 you of** you **196 s.d. Exeunt** Exit

3.2. s.d. [Q: Enter King of Fairies, and Robin goodfellow] **19 mimic** Minnick **38 s.p. [and elsewhere] Puck** Rob **80 I so** I **85 sleep** slippe **213 like** life **220 passionate words** words **250 prayers** praise **260 off** of **299 gentlemen** gentleman **344 s.d. Exit** Exeunt **406 Speak! In** Speake in **426 shalt** shat **451 To your** your

4.1. 5 s.p. [and elsewhere] Bottom Clown **64 off** of **72 o'er** or **81 five** fine **82 ho** howe **116 Seemed** Seeme **127 this is** this **137 s.d. Wind . . . up** they all start vp. Winde hornes **171 saw** see **190 found** fonnd **198 let us** lets **205 to expound** expound **208 a patched** patcht a

4.2. s.d. [Snout, and Starveling] Thisby and the rabble **3 s.p. Starveling** Flut **5 s.p. Flute** Thys [and at ll. 9, 13, 19] **29 no** not

5.1. 34 our Or **107 s.p. [and elsewhere] Theseus** Duke **122 his** this **150 s.d. Exeunt** Exit [and at l. 153 in Q] **155 Snout** Flute **190 up in thee**

now againe   **205 mural down** Moon vsed   **209 s.p. [and elsewhere] Hippolyta** Dutch   **270 gleams** beames   **309 before** before?   **317 warrant** warnd
347 s.p. Bottom Lyon   **366 lion** Lyons   **367 behowls** beholds   **415–416 And
. . . rest** [these lines are transposed in Q]

Shakespeare's Sources

No single source has been discovered that unites the various elements we find in *A Midsummer Night's Dream*, but the four main strands of action can be individually discussed in terms of sources. The four strands are: (1) the marriage of Duke Theseus and Queen Hippolyta, (2) the romantic tribulations and triumphs of the four young lovers, (3) the quarrel of King Oberon and Queen Titania, together with the fairies' manipulations of human affairs, and (4) the "rude mechanicals" and their play of "Pyramus and Thisbe."

For his conception of Theseus, Shakespeare went chiefly to Geoffrey Chaucer's "The Knight's Tale," of which a brief excerpt follows, and to Thomas North's 1579 translation of "The Life of Theseus" in Plutarch's *Lives of the Noble Grecians and Romans*. Chaucer's Theseus is a duke of "wisdom" and "chivalrye," renowned for his conquest of the Amazons and his marriage to Hippolyta. Plutarch provides information concerning Theseus' other conquests (to which Oberon alludes in 2.1.77 ff.), including that of Antiopa. Shakespeare could have learned more about Theseus from Chaucer's *The Legend of Good Women* and from Ovid's *Metamorphoses*. He seems to have blended all or some of these impressions together with his own notion of a noble yet popular Renaissance ruler.

The romantic narrative of the four lovers appears to be original with Shakespeare, although one can find many analogous situations of misunderstanding and rivalry in love. Chaucer's "The Knight's Tale" tells of two friends battling over one woman. Shakespeare's own *The Two Gentlemen of Verona* gives us four lovers, properly matched at first until one of the men shifts his attentions to his friend's ladylove; eventually all is righted when the false lover recovers his senses. Parallel situations arise in Sir Philip Sidney's *Arcadia* (1590) and in Jorge de Montemayor's *Diana* (c. 1559), a source for *The Two Gentlemen*. What Shakespeare adds in *A Midsummer* is the intervention of the fairies in human love affairs.

Shakespeare's knowledge of fairy lore must have been extensive and is hard to trace exactly. Doubtless much of it was from oral traditions about leprechauns, gremlins, and elves, who were thought to cause such mischief as spoiling fermentation or preventing milk from churning into butter; Puck's tricks mentioned in 2.1.34 ff. are derived from such lore. Yet Shakespeare seems to have consulted literary sources as well. In Chaucer's "The Merchant's Tale," Pluto and Proserpina as king and queen of the fairies intervene in the affairs of old January, his young wife May, and her lover Damyan. Fairies appear onstage in John Lyly's *Endymion* (1588), protecting true lovers and tormenting those who are morally tainted. Shakespeare later reflects this tradition in *The Merry Wives of Windsor* (1597–1601). The name Oberon probably comes from the French romance *Huon of Bordeaux* (translated by Lord Berners by about 1540), where Oberon is a dwarfish fairy king from the mysterious East who practices enchantment in a haunted wood. In Edmund Spenser's *The Faerie Queene*, Oberon is the Elfin father of Queen Gloriana (2.10.75–76). Robert Greene's *James IV* (c. 1591) also features Oberon as the fairy king, and a lost play called *Huon of Bordeaux* was performed by Sussex's men, an acting company, at about this same time. The name Titania comes from Ovid's *Metamorphoses*, where it is used as a synonym for both the enchantress Circe and the chaste goddess Diana. The name Titania does not appear in Arthur Golding's translation (1567), suggesting that Shakespeare found it in the original. Puck, or Robin Goodfellow, is essentially the product of oral tradition, although Reginald Scot's *The Discovery of Witchcraft* (1584) discusses Robin in pejorative terms as an incubus or hobgoblin in whom intelligent people no longer believe.

Scot also reports the story of a man who finds an ass's head placed on his shoulders by enchantment. Similar legends of transformation occur in Apuleius' *The Golden Ass* (translated by William Adlington, 1566) and in the well-known story of the ass's ears bestowed by Phoebus Apollo on King Midas for his presumption. Perhaps the most suggestive possible source for Shakespeare's clownish actors, however, is Anthony Munday's play *John a Kent and John a Cumber* (c. 1587–1590). In it a group of rude artisans, led by the intrepid Turnop, stage a ludicrous interlude written by their churchwarden in praise of his millhorse. Turnop's prologue is a medley of lofty comparisons. The entertainment is presented before noble spectators, who are graciously amused. *John a Kent* also features a lot of magic trickery, a boy named Shrimp whose role is comparable to that of Puck, and a multiple love plot.

"Pyramus and Thisbe" itself is based on the *Metamorphoses* (4.55 ff.), as can be seen from the following selection. Other versions Shakespeare may have known include Chaucer's *The Legend of Good Women*, William Griffith's poem *Pyramus and Thisbe* (1562), George Pettie's *A Petite Palace of Pettie His Pleasure* (1576), *A Gorgeous Gallery of Gallant Inventions* (1578), and "A New Sonnet of Pyramus and Thisbe" from Clement Robinson's *A Handful of Pleasant Delights* (1584). Several of these, especially the last three, are bad enough to have given Shakespeare materials to lampoon, though the sweep of his parody goes beyond the particular story of Pyramus and Thisbe. The occasionally stilted phraseology of Golding's translation of *The Metamorphoses* contributed to the fun. According to Kenneth Muir (*Shakespeare's Sources*, 1957), Shakespeare must also have known Thomas Mouffet's *Of the Silkworms and Their Flies* (published 1599, but possibly circulated earlier in manuscript), which contains perhaps the most ridiculous of all versions of the Pyramus and Thisbe story. Shakespeare also appears to be spoofing the inept dramatic style and lame verse of English dramas of the 1560s, 1570s, and 1580s, especially in their treatment of tragic sentiment and high emotion; *Cambises*, *Damon and Pythias*, and *Appius and Virginia* are examples.

The Canterbury Tales
By Geoffrey Chaucer

HERE BEGINNETH THE KNIGHTES TALE

Whilom, as olde stories tellen us,	859
There was a duke that highte Theseus.	860
Of Athens he was lord and governor,	
And in his time swich a conqueror	862
That greater was there none under the sonne.	
Full many a rich country had he wonne;	
What with his wisdom and his chivalrye	
He conquered all the reign of Feminye,	866
That whilom was ycleped Scythia,	867
And weddede the queen Hippolyta	
And brought her home with him in his country	
With muchel glory and great solemnity,	870
And eke her faire suster Emily.	871
And thus with victory and with melody	
Let I this noble duke to Athens ride,	
And all his host in armes him beside.	874
And certes, if it nere too long to hear,	875
I would han told you fully the manner	876
How wonnen was the reign of Feminye	
By Theseus and by his chivalrye,	
And of the greate bataille for the nones	879
Bitwixen Athenes and Amazones,	
And how asseged was Hippolyta,	881
The faire, hardy queen of Scythia,	882
And of the feast that was at hir weddinge,	883
And of the tempest at hir home-cominge;	884
But all that thing I moot as now forbeare.	885
I have, God wot, a large field to eare,	886

859 Whilom once upon a time   **860 highte** was called   **862 swich** such
866 reign of Feminye country of the Amazons   **867 ycleped** called
870 muchel much.   **solemnity** ceremony   **871 eke** also.   **suster** sister
874 him beside beside him   **875 nere too** were not too   **876 would han**
would have   **879 for the nones** in particular   **881 asseged** besieged
882 hardy brave   **883 hir** their (also in l. 884)   **884 tempest** tumult
885 moot must   **886 eare** ear, plow

And weake been the oxen in my plough.
The remnant of the tale is long enough;
I woll nat letten eke none of this route.   889
Let every fellow tell his tale aboute,   890
And let see now who shall the supper winne;   891
And there I left I will again beginne.   892

   This duke, of whom I make mencioun,   893
When he was come almost unto the toun,
In all his weal and in his moste pride,   895
He was war, as he cast his eye aside,   896
Where that there kneeled in the highe waye   897
A company of ladies, tweye and tweye,   898
Each after other, clad in clothes blacke;
But swich a cry and swich a woe they make
That in this world nys creature livinge   901
That hearde swich another waymentinge.   902
And of this cry they nolde nevere stinten   903
Till they the reines of his bridle henten.   904

   "What folk been ye, that at mine home-cominge
Perturben so my feaste with cryinge?"   906
Quod Theseus. "Have ye so great envye   907
Of mine honor, that thus complain and crye?   908
Or who hath you misboden or offended?   909
And telleth me if it may been amended,   910
And why that ye been clothed thus in black?"

   The eldest lady of hem alle spak,   912
When she had swooned with a deadly cheere   913
That it was routhe for to seen and heare,   914
And saide, "Lord, to whom fortune hath given
Victory, and as a conqueror to liven,
Nat grieveth us your glory and your honor,   917
But we beseeken mercy and succor.   918
Have mercy on our woe and our distresse!

---

889 woll nat letten will not hinder.   **route** assembly (the Canterbury pilgrims)   **890 aboute** in succession   **891 let see** let it be seen   **892 there** there where   **893 mencioun** mention   **895 weal** splendor   **896 war** aware.   **aside** to one side   **897 highe waye** highway   **898 tweye and tweye** two by two   **901 nys** is not   **902 waymentinge** lamenting   **903 nolde** would not.   **stinten** stint, cease   **904 reines** reins.   **henten** seized, grasped   **906 feaste** feast, festival celebration   **907–908 envye Of** ill will toward   **909 misboden** harmed   **910 telleth** tell.   **been** be   **912 hem** them   **913 deadly cheere** deathlike appearance   **914 routhe** pity   **917 Nat . . . glory** your glory doesn't grieve us   **918 beseeken** beseech, beg

Some drop of pity, through thy gentillesse,   920
Upon us wretched women let thou falle!
For certes, lord, there is none of us alle   922
That she ne hath been a duchess or a queene.   923
Now be we caitives, as it is well seene.   924
Thanked be Fortune and her false wheel
That none estate assureth to be weel.   926
And certes, lord, to abiden your presence,   927
Here in the temple of the goddess Clemence
We han been waiting all this fourteennight;   929
Now help us, lord, sith it is in thy might . . .   930

[The story of rivalry between Palamon and Arcite bears
only a general resemblance to that of the young lovers in
A Midsummer Night's Dream, but when Chaucer and the
Knight return to an account of revels and tournaments in
honor of the wedding of Theseus and Hippolyta, the splendor of the Athenian court is not unlike that in Act 5 of
Shakespeare's play.]

The Canterbury Tales of Chaucer date from 1387–1400. This sparingly mod-
ernized selection from "The Knight's Tale" is based on the Ellesmere manuscript, Ellesmere 26 c. 12, now in the Huntington Library, San Marino,
California. Group A, ll. 859–930.

In the following, departures from the original text appear in boldface; the
original readings follow in roman:

868 weddede wedded   **876 han told you** yow haue toold   **897 highe waye** weye

920 gentillesse courtesy, good breeding   **922 certes** certainly   **923 ne hath**
has not   **924 caitives** caitiffs, wretches   **926 none . . . weel** i.e., no human
prosperity can assure itself of long felicity   **927 abiden** await
929 fourteennight fortnight   **930 sith** since

Metamorphoses
By Ovid
Translated by Arthur Golding

BOOK 4

Within the town (of whose huge walls so monstrous
   high and thick
The fame is given Semiramis for making them of
   brick)   68
Dwelt hard together two young folk, in houses joined
   so near   69
That under all one roof well nigh both twain con-
   veyèd were.   70
The name of him was Pyramus, and Thisbe called
   was she.
So fair a man in all the East was none alive as he,
Nor ne'er a woman, maid, nor wife in beauty like to
   her.
This neighborhood bred acquaintance first; this
   neighborhood first did stir   74
The secret sparks; this neighborhood first an en-
   trance in did show
For love to come to that to which it afterward did
   grow.
   And if that right had taken place, they had been
   man and wife;
But still their parents went about to let which, for
   their life,   78
They could not let. For both their hearts with equal
   flame did burn.
No man was privy to their thoughts; and, for to serve
   their turn,
Instead of talk, they usèd signs. The closelier they
   suppressed

68 Semiramis the Queen of Assyria, 810–806 B.C., who was reputed to have
ordered the building of the walls of Babylon   **69 hard together** hard by
70 conveyèd taken, led, placed   **74 neighborhood** friendly relations between
neighbors   **78 still** always.   **let which** hinder that which.   **for their life** even
if their lives depended on it

The fire of love, the fiercer still it ragèd in their
   breast.
  The wall that parted house from house had riven
    therein a cranny,
Which shrunk at making of the wall. This fault, not
   marked of any   84
Of many hundred years before—what doth not love
   espy?—
These lovers first of all found out and made a way
   whereby
To talk together secretly; and through the same did
   go
Their loving whisperings, very light and safely, to and
   fro.
  Now, as at one side Pyramus, and Thisbe on the
    tother,
Stood often drawing one of them the pleasant breath
   from other,
"O thou envious wall!" they said. "Why lett'st thou
   lovers thus?   91
What matter were it if that thou permitted both of us
In arms each other to embrace? Or if thou think that
   this
Were overmuch, yet mightest thou at least make
   room to kiss.
And yet thou shalt not find us churls; we think our-
   selves in debt
For the same piece of courtesy, in vouching safe to let   96
Our sayings to our friendly ears thus freely come and
   go."
Thus having, where they stood in vain, complainèd of
   their woe,
When night drew near they bade adieu, and each
   gave kisses sweet
Unto the parget on their side, the which did never
   meet.   100
  Next morning with her cheerful light had driven
    the stars aside,

---

84 shrunk i.e., resulted from shrinkage **91 lett'st thou** do you hinder
96 vouching safe vouchsafing, permitting **100 parget** roughcast, plaster
usually made of lime and cow-dung. **the which** i.e., which kisses

And Phoebus with his burning beams the dewy grass
   had dried.
These lovers at their wonted place by foreappoint-
   ment met;
Where, after much complaint and moan, they cove-
   nanted to get
Away from such as watchèd them, and in the evening
   late
To steal out of their fathers' house and eke the city
   gate.   106
And to th' intent that in the fields they strayed not
   up and down,   107
They did agree at Ninus' tomb to meet without the
   town   108
And tarry underneath a tree that by the same did
   grow,
Which was a fair high mulberry with fruit as white
   as snow,
Hard by a cool and trickling spring. This bargain
   pleased them both,
And so daylight, which to their thought away but
   slowly go'th,
Did in the ocean fall to rest, and night from thence
   doth rise.
   As soon as darkness once was come, straight
     Thisbe did devise
A shift to wind her out of doors, that none that were
   within   115
Perceivèd her, and muffling her with clothes about
   her chin
That no man might discern her face, to Ninus' tomb
   she came
Unto the tree, and sat her down there underneath the
   same.
   Love made her bold. But see the chance! There
     comes, besmeared with blood
About the chaps, a lioness, all foaming, from the
   wood,

106 eke also   **107 strayed not** would not stray   **108 Ninus** husband of
Semiramis, mythical founder of Nineveh. (Nineveh and Babylon appear to
have been confused.)   **without** outside   **115 shift** device.   **wind her** move by
sinuous course

From slaughter lately made of kine, to stanch her
    bloody thirst   121
With water of the foresaid spring. Whom Thisbe,
    spying first
Afar by moonlight, thereupon with fearful steps gan
    fly,
And in a dark and irksome cave did hide herself
    thereby.
And as she fled away for haste she let her mantle fall,
The which for fear she left behind, not looking back
    at all.
    Now, when the cruel lioness her thirst had
        stanchèd well,
In going to the wood she found the slender weed that
    fell   128
From Thisbe, which with bloody teeth in pieces she
    did tear.
    The night was somewhat further spent ere Pyramus
        came there,
Who, seeing in this subtle sand the print of lion's
    paw,   131
Waxed pale for fear. But when also the bloody cloak
    he saw
All rent and torn, "One night," he said, "shall lovers
    two confound!   133
Of which long life deservèd she of all that live on
    ground.   134
My soul deserves of this mischance the peril for to
    bear.
I, wretch, have been the death of thee, which to this
    place of fear
Did cause thee in the night to come, and came not
    here before.
My wicked limbs and wretched guts with cruel teeth
    therefore
Devour ye, O ye lions all that in this rock do dwell!

---

121 kine cattle. **stanch** slake   **128 weed** garment   **131 subtle** i.e., capable
of preserving an indistinct impression   **133 confound** destroy   **134 Of . . .
ground** one of whom (Thisbe) deserved long life more than any other person
on earth

But cowards use to wish for death." The slender
   weed that fell   140
From Thisbe up he takes and straight doth bear it to
   the tree   141
Which was appointed erst the place of meeting for to
   be.   142
And when he had bewept and kissed the garment
   which he knew,
"Receive thou my blood too!" quoth he, and there-
   withal he drew
His sword, the which among his guts he thrust, and
   by and by
Did draw it from the bleeding wound, beginning for
   to die,
And cast himself upon his back. The blood did spin
   on high;
As when a conduit pipe is cracked, the water bursting
   out
Doth shoot itself a great way off and pierce the air
   about.
The leaves that were upon the tree, besprinkled with
   his blood,
Were dyèd black. The root also, bestainèd as it stood,
A deep dark purple color straight upon the berries
   cast.
   Anon, scarce ridded of her fear with which she was
   aghast,
For doubt of disappointing him comes Thisbe forth
   in haste   154
And for her lover looks about, rejoicing for to tell
How hardly she had scaped that night the danger
   that befell.   156
And as she knew right well the place and fashion of
   the tree,
As which she saw so late before, even so, when she
   did see   158

---

140 use to make it a practice to. (Cowards only pretend to be ready to die;
brave persons act.) **141 straight** straightway, at once **142 erst** at an earlier
time **154 doubt** fear **156 hardly** scarcely **158 As . . . before** which she
had seen so recently

The color of the berries turned, she was uncertain
   whether
It were the tree at which they both agreed to meet
    together.
   While in this doubtful stound she stood, she cast
    her eye aside,   161
And there, beweltered in his blood, her lover she
   espied
Lie sprawling with his dying limbs; at which she
   started back
And lookèd pale as any box. A shuddering through
   her strack,   164
Even like the sea which suddenly with whizzing noise
   doth move
When with a little blast of wind it is but touched
   above.
But, when approaching nearer him, she knew it was
   her love,
She beat her breast, she shriekèd out, she tare her
   golden hairs,   168
And, taking him between her arms, did wash his
    wounds with tears.
   She meynt her weeping with his blood, and kissing
    all his face,   170
Which now became as cold as ice, she cried in woeful
   case,
"Alas! What chance, my Pyramus, hath parted thee
   and me?
Make answer, O my Pyramus. It is thy Thisb, even she
Whom thou dost love most heartily, that speaketh
   unto thee.
Give ear, and raise thy heavy head!" He, hearing
   Thisbe's name,
Lift up his dying eyes and, having seen her, closed
   the same.   176
   But when she knew her mantle there and saw his
    scabbard lie

---

161 stound pang, shock; difficult time   **164 pale as any box** i.e., ashen,
pallid, like the color of boxwood.   **strack** struck   **168 tare** tore   **170 meynt**
(past tense of *meng*), mingled   **176 Lift** lifted

Without the sword: "Unhappy man! Thy love hath
   made thee die.
Thy love," she said, "hath made thee slay thyself.
   This hand of mine
Is strong enough to do the like. My love no less than
   thine
Shall give me force to work my wound. I will pursue
   thee dead,   181
And, wretched woman as I am, it shall of me be said
That, like as of thy death I was the only cause and
   blame,   183
So am I thy companion eke and partner in the same. 184
For death, which only could, alas! asunder part us
   twain,   185
Shall never so dissever us but we will meet again.
   "And you the parents of us both, most wretched
      folk alive,
Let this request that I shall make in both our names
   belive   188
Entreat you to permit that we, whom chaste and
   steadfast love
And whom even death hath joined in one, may, as it
   doth behoove,
In one grave be together laid. And thou, unhappy
   tree,
Which shroudest now the corpse of one, and shalt
   anon through me
Shroud two, of this same slaughter hold the sicker
   signs for aye.   193
Black be the color of thy fruit, and mourning-like
   alway,
Such as the murder of us twain may evermore
   bewray."   195
   This said, she took the sword, yet warm with
      slaughter of her love,
And setting it beneath her breast, did to her heart it
   shove.

---

181 work inflict   **183 like as** just as   **184 eke** also   **185 only** alone
188 belive urgently   **193 sicker** sure.   **aye** ever   **195 bewray** reveal

Her prayer with the gods and with their parents took
    effect.
For when the fruit is throughly ripe, the berry is
    bespecked,   199
With color tending to a black. And that which after
    fire   200
Remainèd, rested in one tomb, as Thisbe did desire.

———————————

The text is based on *The XV Books of P. Ovidius Naso, Entitled Metamorphoses. Translated out of Latin into English meter by Arthur Golding*. London, 1567. This is the first edition of Golding's translation.

199 throughly thoroughly   **200 fire** i.e., cremation

Further Reading

Barber, C. L. "May Games and Metamorphoses on a Midsummer Night." *Shakespeare's Festive Comedy*. Princeton, N.J.: Princeton Univ. Press, 1959. Barber explores how the social forms of Elizabethan holiday and celebration contribute to the dramatic form of Shakespeare's comedy. *A Midsummer Night's Dream* uses folk customs and aristocratic pageantry to organize its contrasts between reason and feeling, waking and dreaming, enabling the play to acknowledge the creative power of the human imagination while simultaneously recognizing that its creations are often "more strange than true."

Bevington, David. " 'But We Are Spirits of Another Sort': The Dark Side of Love and Magic in *A Midsummer Night's Dream*." *Medieval and Renaissance Studies* 7 (1975): 80–92. Bevington draws attention to the tension in the play "between comic reassurance and the suggestion of something dark and threatening." In pointing to the play's disturbing currents of libidinous sexuality, Bevington recognizes but distances himself from the position of Jan Kott (see below), arguing that the play successfully effects a reconciliation between the dark and affirmative sides of love—reconciliation that finds its symbol in the image of Titania and the ass's head.

Calderwood, James L. *"A Midsummer Night's Dream:* Art's Illusory Sacrifice." *Shakespearean Metadrama*. Minneapolis: Univ. of Minnesota Press, 1971. In Calderwood's metadramatic perspective, *A Midsummer Night's Dream* is the comedy that most fully participates in Shakespeare's ongoing dramatic exploration of the nature, function, and value of art. The characters' experience *in* the play mirrors the audience's experience *of* the play, as each is challenged to discover reality through illusions. Dream thereby becomes an analogue of the drama itself, a drama "in which man sees his dreams."

Dent, R. W. "Imagination in *A Midsummer Night's Dream*." *Shakespeare Quarterly* 15, no. 2 (1964), 115–129. Although Theseus indiscriminately lumps together lunatics, lovers, and poets, Shakespeare, Dent argues, carefully dis-

tinguishes between the role of imagination in love and in
art. This distinction, demonstrated in Shakespeare's handling of the mechanicals' play, confirms *A Midsummer
Night's Dream*'s unity of design, while offering us Shakespeare's own "Defense of Dramatic Poesy."

Evans, Bertrand. "All Shall Be Well: The Way Found."
Shakespeare's Comedies. Oxford: Clarendon Press, 1960.
Evans explores Shakespeare's handling of the different
levels of awareness and understanding that characters
display in the play. Oberon comes closest to the audience's privileged vantage point, while Bottom, who
seems to have a wonderful resistance to understanding,
is most distant. *A Midsummer Night's Dream* departs
from the usual pattern of Shakespeare's comedies in that
the denouement does not raise the characters to a level of
awareness equal to that of the audience.

Fender, Stephen. *Shakespeare: "A Midsummer Night's
Dream."* London: Edward Arnold, 1968. In a brief (64
pages), engaging book, Fender argues that provocative
moral ambiguities emerge from the play's unusual structural complexity. We are constantly made aware of ten-
sions and contradictions in the depiction of characters
and settings, even in blind love itself. The play demands
of us what Keats called Negative Capability: the ability to
accept multiplicity, mystery, and doubt without reaching
out for the illusory comforts of certainty and fact.

Garber, Marjorie B. "Spirits of Another Sort: *A Midsummer
Night's Dream.*" *Dream in Shakespeare: From Metaphor
to Metamorphosis*. New Haven and London: Yale Univ.
Press, 1974. The dreams in *A Midsummer Night's Dream*,
according to Garber, function both to articulate the central theme of the play—imaginative transformation—and
to provide a model for the play's construction. Dreams
become emblems of the visionary experience itself, forc-
ing characters as well as the audience out of familiar
habits of mind into new modes of perception and understanding.

Girard, René. "Myth and Ritual in Shakespeare: *A Midsummer Night's Dream.*" In *Textual Strategies: Perspectives in Post-Structuralist Criticism*, ed. Josué V. Harari.
Ithaca, N.Y.: Cornell Univ. Press, 1979. Girard argues that

in the confusions of the forest the lovers lose their identities because of their insistence on loving "through another's eyes." In the destructiveness of this mimetic desire Girard finds not only the theme of this play but also the "basic Shakespearean relationship" of all the comedies and tragedies.

Granville-Barker, Harley. *"A Midsummer Night's Dream."* In *More Prefaces to Shakespeare,* ed. Edward M. Moore. Princeton, N.J.: Princeton Univ. Press, 1974. Granville-Barker, writing as both critic and director, addresses the special problems raised in producing *A Midsummer Night's Dream* in a world accustomed to the realistic conventions of the modern theater. His analysis focuses on how the clowns, fairies, dance, and music could be handled effectively and convincingly, and he urges that the stage business be subordinated to Shakespeare's overriding emphasis on the play's language.

Kermode, Frank. "The Mature Comedies." In *Early Shakespeare,* ed. John Russell Brown and Bernard Harris. Stratford-upon-Avon Studies 3. London: Edward Arnold, 1961. For Kermode, the play, rich in intellectual content and sophisticated in design, is Shakespeare's "best comedy." His essay examines how Shakespeare's thematic preoccupation with blind love draws upon the philosophical treatment of this idea in the works of Macrobius, Apuleius, and Bruno. The result, Kermode argues, is a complex and serious work of art, intellectually and theatrically satisfying in its comic achievement.

Kott, Jan. "Titania and the Ass's Head." *Shakespeare Our Contemporary,* trans. Boleslaw Taborski. New York: Doubleday, 1964. In Kott's dark vision of love and human relations in *A Midsummer Night's Dream,* the night in the forest releases an "erotic madness" of perversity and obsession that is abruptly censured by the coming of day. Love is revealed as undignified and degrading, denying the lovers even their individuality in their compulsive behavior.

Leggatt, Alexander. *"A Midsummer Night's Dream." Shakespeare's Comedy of Love.* London: Methuen, 1974. In a sensitive essay, Leggatt explores Shakespeare's skillful arrangement of characters and perspectives. The play, he argues, achieves its imaginative power through a series of comic contrasts that confirms both the folly and the integrity of each group of characters.

Merchant, W. Moelwyn. *"A Midsummer Night's Dream:* A Visual Recreation." In *Early Shakespeare,* ed. John Russell Brown and Bernard Harris. Stratford-upon-Avon Studies 3. London: Edward Arnold, 1961. The play, which demanded the full range of the theatrical possibilities of the Elizabethan stage, in the ensuing centuries has received treatments that have tended to oversimplify the play to achieve certain desired theatrical effects. Merchant, surveying this stage history, concludes that directors have generally failed to integrate the undeniable charm of the fairy world with the more unsettling side of the play.

Montrose, Louis Adrian. " 'Shaping Fantasies': Figurations of Gender and Power in Elizabethan Culture." *Representations* 1, no. 2 (1983): 61–94. Montrose is interested in the relationship of Elizabethan drama to the culture that produced it, especially in how Shakespeare's plays reproduce and challenge existing social structures. His discussion of how the world of Queen Elizabeth's England and the world of *A Midsummer Night's Dream* are mutually illuminating focuses on questions of power, patriarchy, and sexual politics, concluding that in a double sense the play is a *"creation* of Elizabethan culture."

Olson, Paul A. *"A Midsummer Night's Dream* and the Meaning of Court Marriage." *ELH* 24 (1957): 95–119. Rpt. in *Shakespeare's Comedies: An Anthology of Modern Criticism,* ed. Laurence Lerner. Baltimore: Penguin, 1967. Olson calls attention to one possible occasion of the play's first performance (the celebration of a courtly marriage) as a sign of its seriousness and sophistication. He surveys Renaissance ideas about love and art to discover the principles that organize the play's elaborate formal contrasts, examining how the language and structure of the play "work together to make luminous a traditional understanding of marriage" that mirrors and reinforces the social order.

Selbourne, David. *The Making of "A Midsummer Night's Dream."* London: Methuen, 1982. Selbourne's account of the development of Peter Brook's Royal Shakespeare

Company production of *A Midsummer Night's Dream* (1970) offers insight into the creative interplay of director, cast, and text that resulted in this remarkable and influential production.

Young, David P. *Something of Great Constancy: The Art of "A Midsummer Night's Dream."* New Haven, Conn.: Yale Univ. Press, 1966. In this book-length study of the carefully constructed and interlocking harmonies of the play, Young examines Shakespeare's fusion of the courtly and popular material of his sources, his integration of stylistic and structural elements, and his manipulation of audience response. For Young, the transforming power of the imagination allows the play's apparently discordant elements to grow into "something of great constancy."

Memorable Lines

The course of true love never did run smooth.
(LYSANDER   1.1.134)

So quick bright things come to confusion.
(LYSANDER   1.1.149)

Love looks not with the eyes, but with the mind,
And therefore is winged Cupid painted blind.
(HELENA   1.1.234–235)

. . ."The most lamentable comedy and most cruel death of
Pyramus and Thisbe."   (QUINCE   1.2.11–12)

Over hill, over dale,
  Thorough bush, thorough brier,
Over park, over pale,
  Thorough flood, thorough fire. . . .   (FAIRY   2.1.2–5)

Ill met by moonlight, proud Titania.   (OBERON   2.1.60)

I'll put a girdle round about the earth
In forty minutes.   (PUCK   2.1.175–176)

I know a bank where the wild thyme blows,
Where oxlips and the nodding violet grows,
Quite overcanopied with luscious woodbine,
With sweet muskroses and with eglantine.
(OBERON   2.1.249–252)

You spotted snakes with double tongue,
  Thorny hedgehogs, be not seen;
Newts and blindworms, do no wrong,
  Come not near our Fairy Queen.   (FAIRY   2.2.9–12)

Lord, what fools these mortals be!   (PUCK   3.2.115)

And though she be but little, she is fierce.
(HELENA   3.2.325)

My Oberon! What visions have I seen!
Methought I was enamored of an ass. (TITANIA 4.1.75–76)

The lunatic, the lover, and the poet
Are of imagination all compact.
One sees more devils than vast hell can hold;
That is the madman. The lover, all as frantic,
Sees Helen's beauty in a brow of Egypt.
The poet's eye, in a fine frenzy rolling,
Doth glance from heaven to earth, from earth to heaven;
And as imagination bodies forth
The forms of things unknown, the poet's pen
Turns them to shapes and gives to airy nothing
A local habitation and a name. (THESEUS 5.1.7–17)

. . . the true beginning of our end. (PROLOGUE 5.1.111)

The iron tongue of midnight hath told twelve.
Lovers, to bed, 'tis almost fairy time.

(THESEUS 5.1.358–359)

If we shadows have offended,
Think but this, and all is mended,
That you have but slumbered here
While these visions did appear. (PUCK 5.1.419–422)

Contributors

DAVID BEVINGTON, Phyllis Fay Horton Professor of Humanities at the University of Chicago, is editor of *The Complete Works of Shakespeare* (Scott, Foresman, 1980) and of *Medieval Drama* (Houghton Mifflin, 1975). His latest critical study is *Action Is Eloquence: Shakespeare's Language of Gesture* (Harvard University Press, 1984).

DAVID SCOTT KASTAN, Professor of English and Comparative Literature at Columbia University, is the author of *Shakespeare and the Shapes of Time* (University Press of New England, 1982).

JAMES HAMMERSMITH, Associate Professor of English at Auburn University, has published essays on various facets of Renaissance drama, including literary criticism, textual criticism, and printing history.

ROBERT KEAN TURNER, Professor of English at the University of Wisconsin–Milwaukee, is a general editor of the New Variorum Shakespeare (Modern Language Association of America) and a contributing editor to *The Dramatic Works in the Beaumont and Fletcher Canon* (Cambridge University Press, 1966–).

JAMES SHAPIRO, who coedited the bibliographies, is Assistant Professor of English at Columbia University.

✠

JOSEPH PAPP, one of the most important forces in theater today, is the founder and producer of the New York Shakespeare Festival, America's largest and most prolific theatrical institution. Since 1954 Mr. Papp has produced or directed all but one of Shakespeare's plays—in Central Park, in schools, off and on Broadway, and at the Festival's permanent home, The Public Theater. He has also produced such award-winning plays and musical works as *Hair, A Chorus Line, Plenty,* and *The Mystery of Edwin Drood,* among many others.

Bantam Drama Classics

☐ 21354   Sophocles: Complete Plays $3.95
☐ 21363   Euripides: Ten Plays $3.95
☐ 21343   Aristophanes: Complete Plays $4.50
☐ 21280   Henrik Ibsen: Four Great Plays $2.95
☐ 21360   Rostand: Cyrano De Bergerac $1.95
☐ 21211   Anton Chekhov: Five Major
                Plays $2.95

Buy them at your local bookstore or use this page to order.

- -

Bantam Books, Dept. CL5, 414 East Golf Road,
Des Plaines, IL 60016

Please send me the books I have checked above. I am enclosing
$_____ (Please add $2.00 to cover postage and handling.)
Send check or money order—no cash or C.O.D.s please.

Mr/Ms _____

Address _____

City/State _____ Zip _____

CL5—10/89

Please allow four to six weeks for delivery.
Prices and availability subject to change without notice.

the BANTAM Shakespeare

Bantam is proud to announce an important new edition of:

The Complete Works Of William Shakespeare

Featuring:

*The complete texts with modern spelling and punctuation

*Vivid, readable introductions by noted Shakespearean scholar David Bevington

*New forewords by Joseph Papp, renowned producer, director, and founder of the New York Shakespeare Festival

*Stunning, original cover art by Mark English, the most awarded illustrator in the history of the Society of Illustrators

*Photographs from some of the most celebrated performances by the New York Shakespeare Festival

*Complete source materials, notes, and annotated bibliographies based on the latest scholarships

*Stage histories for each play

ACCESSIBLE * AUTHORITATIVE * COMPLETE

SHAKESPEARE
The Complete works in 29 Volumes

THE COMPLETE WORKS IN 29 VOLUMES
Edited, with introductions by David Bevington
•Forewords by Joseph Papp